DON'T SAY PLEASE: THE ORAL HISTORY OF DIE KREUZEN

A Feral House Book

ISBN 978-1627311649

fh

FERAL HOUSE
1240 W Sims Way #124
Port Townsend WA 98368
www.feralhouse.com
info@feralhouse.com

Designed by Ron Kretsch

Cover photo by Jennifer Leazer

Collaged photos on pages 4–5 and 222–223 by Marty Graham,
Barbara Herring, Kevin Hutchison, Scott Lubic, Corey Rusk,
and various unknown photographers.

Don't Say Please
The Oral History of die kreuzen

By Sahan Jayasuriya

Die Kreuzen rip through a live set early on, c. 1983.
Photo: Kevin Hutchison.

FOREWORD

by Steven Blush

DIE KREUZEN, FROM THE BLUE-COLLAR, INDUSTRIAL HUB OF Milwaukee, Wisconsin, represented the "meat and potatoes" America echoed in Midwest hardcore. But you can keep your "Brew City" bratwurst and frozen custard shops; I'll take the greatest band most people have never heard.

Their story began in a town 93 miles west of Chicago—Rockford, Illinois—as a teenage Psychedelic Furs–style new wave band called the Stellas, who relocated to Milwaukee and played "Punk Nights" at the long-since-gentrified waterfront taverns. The band members got inspired by the speed and fury of the new American hardcore explosion in 1981 and rechristened themselves Die Kreuzen, grammatically incorrect German for "the crosses." They came to cult attention with appearances on seminal Midwest compilations like *Charred Remains, The Master Tape,* and *America's Dairyland,* none of which are commercially available today.

I was lucky enough to experience their hardcore fury firsthand while I was on the road with the Washington, D.C., noise band No Trend—both bands opening for Dead Kennedys—and Die Kreuzen were so damn good that we arrived early for the gigs on four or five occasions just to watch their blistering soundchecks. There, I traded records for a copy of their classic six-song 7" EP *Cows & Beer* (a salute to their home state's agrarian-Teutonic heritage), which was so intense that thirty-plus years later, I chose to put the song "Think for Me" on the *American Hardcore* film soundtrack album.

The core four—vocalist Dan Kubinski on vocals, guitarist Brian Egeness, bassist Keith Brammer, and drummer Erik Tunison—created some of the first raging alternative rock on Touch and Go Records, particularly on 1986's *October File* and 1988's *Century Days*, which hugely inspired groundbreaking bands such as Soundgarden, Mudhoney, and Voivod. During that time period, I booked Die Kreuzen in New York City on their *October File* tour and can honestly say that at that point in musical history they were the best underground band in America: a beautiful, sloppy mess of surly, noisy genius. I loved what they did and how loudly they did it.

Befitting their Midwestern demeanor, these were some of the nicest guys who were great to hang out with. They all rate mention, but Kubinski was always cool as hell, and Brammer is one of the nicest guys you'll meet in this awful industry.

Almost thirty-five years later, Die Kreuzen finally receive their moment of validation. The book in your hands, *Don't Say Please: The Oral History of Die Kreuzen* by Sahan Jayasuriya, is a labor of love. This book won't appear on mainstream bestseller lists or win fancy literary prizes. That's not the point. All that matters is that this story finally gets told in their own words. Sit back and enjoy the read.

— Steven Blush

Author/filmmaker, *American Hardcore*

New York, 2025

Dan Kubinski caught in the act of doing what he does best, c. 1983. Photo: Kevin Hutchison.

Keith, mid-kick, c. 1986. Photo: Debbie Pastor.

INTRODUCTION

THE AMERICAN MIDWEST IS UNDERESTIMATED BY THE REST OF the country, not to mention the rest of the world. Travel internationally as a Midwesterner and you'll be fortunate if you're able to explain your place of residence in relation to Chicago.

To many, the Midwest is little more than cows and beer, but even the slightest amount of research reveals far more depth and innovation than what is usually attributed to us. Frank Lloyd Wright, Amelia Earhart, Ray Croc, and Betty Friedan were all from "flyover states," ironically, a term that could not exist if not for the work of two brothers from Dayton, Ohio. The region is the home of an array of different inventions: the supercomputer, the pacemaker, sliced bread, the zipper, and Kool-Aid.

One of the strongest examples of this ingenuity is apparent in the region's music. In addition to being the site where multi-track recording was invented, the Midwest is home to some of the most important and innovative musicians of the last half-century—Bob Dylan, Parliament-Funkadelic, Devo, and Madonna all came from or at some point called the Midwest their home. Their efforts aren't always forgotten, though; their backgrounds are. At best, they are considered isolated cases.

But that's just scratching the surface, as the aforementioned acts are all million-sellers, critically lauded, or some combination of the two. Dig deeper into music in the Midwest and one will quickly see that its impact spans a variety of genres and locales, among them punk rock and its many offshoots.

When punk's first wave hit in the mid to late '70s, itself influenced heavily by the Midwest's own MC5 and the Stooges, it wasn't long before disaffected musicians formed punk rock bands. When punk eventually gave way to hardcore, the Midwest was right there at the forefront, birthing one of the genre's most significant labels, Touch and Go, as well as bands like Negative Approach from Detroit, Hüsker Dü from Minneapolis, and a four-piece from Milwaukee called Die Kreuzen.

IT'S 2006, I'M TWENTY-ONE YEARS OLD, AND I'VE RECENTLY begun working at Atomic Records in Milwaukee, an institution in both the city itself and nationwide. I'd been shopping there since my early teen years, both excited by the prospect of finding new and obscure releases and intimidated by its knowledgeable and uber-cool staff. Today, though, it's more intimidation than excitement. I have to work alone with the store owner Rich, something I had yet to do this early in my time there.

"So you're into hardcore, are ya?" Rich says to me in an attempt to break the ice.

"Uh, yeah, I'm into hardcore," I sheepishly reply.

"Well then surely you like Die Kreuzen," he says back to me.

"Die Kreuzen?" I say back. "Aren't they that German band?"

"No," he says back with a laugh. "That's Einstürzende Neubauten, Sahan."

"Oh, right, right," I say, slightly embarrassed.

"I should send you home for an offense like that," Rich says jokingly. "But I don't wanna cover your shift."

Then, Rich reaches into a bin of seven-inches, thumbs around a bit, pulls out a record, and hands it to me.

"Take this home and give it a spin. They're from here and they're great," he says casually. The shop didn't have a working turntable hooked up at the time, and his nonchalant nature did little more than mildly pique my interest.

A few hours later, I walk home, put my bag down, and take out the record. It was a pretty simple design, a black and white image printed on simple yellow cardstock, with an image of a crucifix headstone in a pasture, surrounded by barbed wire and other tombstones loosely around it. On the backside, an even more sparse continuation of the pasture, with an illustration of a cow. I had seen this record before at various punk and metal record shops, but never thought twice to give it a listen.

I took the record out of the sleeve, put it on my turntable, placed the needle down on the first track, and walked away to go make dinner. A guitar chord rang out, a voice sneered, "Yo mama," a jet-paced bassline appeared, and in less than ten seconds the music exploded out of my speakers. Instantly, I turned off my kitchen sink and with dripping wet hands went back to the turntable, where I stood, staring at the record in complete awe. Every song was loud, fast, and razor-sharp. I flipped the record and continued to just stand there, listening, in complete shock. The thought crossed my mind so vividly, I may as well have said it out loud.

"Why did it take me so long to hear this band?"

I had discovered hardcore punk at age fifteen after seeing a local band rip through a ten-songs-in-eight-minutes set in a basement. I was familiar with late-'90s acts on labels like Victory and Equal Vision, but this was something else, something I had been waiting to discover. The drummer openly admitted that they were merely doing their best impersonation of a band called Minor Threat, and that was all the information I needed. I dove headfirst into the early Dischord and SST catalogs, which lead me to other labels like Gravity and Ebullition. By the time I had started working at Atomic, my familiarity with Touch and Go came in the form of their output from the '90s—records by the Jesus Lizard, Slint, Blonde Redhead, and Brainiac. Their early output was a blind spot for me, unaware as I was of the label's seismic contribution to the first wave of hardcore punk. Arrogantly, I figured I had heard a good chunk of what was important from that period. Clearly, I was very wrong.

I eventually found the now-legendary public-access footage of Die Kreuzen and their self-titled album, only further perplexing me. To me, they were not too far off from things like the Germs, Bad Brains and Void, acts that I had found through word of mouth or whose logos were inescapable. It puzzled me as to why Die Kreuzen's music wasn't mentioned as frequently as theirs.

It stuck with me for a very long time, and as I slowly got to know some of the band members, my curiosity about their history only increased. They were down to earth and talkative, having shopped and previously worked at the store for years. I'd often ask them random questions about their influences and experiences as a band, as there was very little information about them to be found at the time. The more I learned, though, the more questions I ended up having.

A few years after working there, I started to write about music locally. After writing a short-form retrospective about Die Kreuzen for a now-defunct Milwaukee publication, the band members approached me about doing something longer and more in depth. A book about their history was something they often thought about doing but never actually pursued.

I took this project on in 2015 with the goal of sharing the story of Die Kreuzen with anyone who cared to read it. Years of research and interviews yielded a sizable archive of material to draw from. Though it took me nearly a decade to finish, let me cite the words of my dear friend and mentor, the late Dr. Martin Jack Rosenblum.

"I think that for every half hour worth of quality teaching, there should be at least a solid decade's worth of learning."

What you hold in your hands is the result of a decade's worth of learning. Enjoy. ●

Nice Boys from the Midwest

IT'S DEBATABLE WHETHER DIE KREUZEN COULD HAVE EVER happened at any other time or in any other place besides the American Midwest during the 1980s. The foursome were fortunate to have grown up in such a musically rich time, where some of the most significant music in history was playing in real time. Had it been earlier or later and in a completely different part of the country, one could argue that the band would have turned out much differently or even failed to exist at all.

Their story, like many others, starts in suburban America. Many bands are made up of childhood friends who grew up together, attended the same high school or college, or were in overlapping social circles, and this is partially true of Die Kreuzen. Keith Brammer and Erik Tunison were born in an upper-middle-class suburb of Milwaukee called Brookfield. Dan Kubinski and Brian Egeness were born in the working-class city of Rockford, Illinois, near the Wisconsin border. While only separated by ninety miles, their respective childhoods were different but had common touchstones.

In hindsight, Die Kreuzen's eventual formation feels inevitable: four wildly talented individuals with shared influences who were seemingly made to play music together. However, the members of the band were living typical lives of elementary-school-aged kids.

Brian Egeness (Guitarist, Die Kreuzen): I was born in Rockford, Illinois, in 1962, which at the time was a small middle-class town. I had an average upbringing, and honestly there wasn't much to do in Rockford. I didn't have too many friends, so I instead focused on music, which grabbed me at an early age.

Keith Brammer (Bassist, Die Kreuzen): I was born in 1962 in Brookfield, Wisconsin. Erik Tunison and I grew up about a quarter of a mile from each other. We knew each other all through grade school into junior high, though I can't recall specifically how we met.

Erik Tunison (Drummer, Die Kreuzen): Keith and I started hanging out in the fourth grade. We had a bunch of classes together. I remember Miss Kling gave both of us Fs in something. I was terrified to go home that day but I remember thinking, "Yeah, but she gave Keith one, she must be just giving these things away." Keith used to say, "Yeah, well, Erik got one too!"

From a young age, all four members were interested in a broad range of music. This musical eclecticism eventually proved useful once they began playing music of their own. At this point, though, it was simply about being open to a variety of sounds.

Keith: The first record I ever got was a Monkees 45 that I bought at a church sale. That and the Partridge Family and stuff. Music was something I was always interested in.

Erik: The first cool record I bought was *Physical Graffiti*. I probably had a Three Dog Night record or two before that, but I was also really into music in grade school. I remember when "Hello Goodbye" was a hit in 1967. I was four years old! I distinctly remember loving Creedence Clearwater Revival at the time.

Dan Kubinski (vocalist, Die Kreuzen): I inherited my father's throwaway 45s when I was pretty young, and I remember having my little wire rack that held them all in my bedroom. There were a bunch of Creedence Clearwater Revival singles in there and those really blew my mind, especially "Travelin' Band." I loved the screaming in that one. I got twenty-five cents a week for allowance back then, and I went every week to Kmart and bought a new 45 with it.

Keith: Music was huge. I was handicapped by the fact that a) I lived in Brookfield and b) I had no older brothers or sisters, so I kind of had to figure things out for myself. All of my friends were into music, and different kinds of music at that. We liked oddball stuff. None of us liked REO Speedwagon or Styx or Fleetwood Mac. We were into Syd Barrett–era Pink Floyd, Brian Eno, and the *Nuggets* compilation. We were super into *Nuggets*. That comp changed our lives. It was a watershed thing.

Erik: *Nuggets* changed everything—that was a heck of a comp.

Keith: It was the one thing we could bring to our friends' older brothers parties, and they would be really into it. Anything else they didn't wanna hear, but that comp was great.

Erik: Of course we loved Eno, Bowie, and T. Rex. I was working my way through the Deep Purple back catalogue and digging into Peter Hammill and Van der Graaf Generator.

Keith: Erik was the point person on Van der Graaf, he was way into it.

Erik: We weren't really interested in anything that was in the mainstream. You might listen to the radio and tape stuff that you liked off of there. There was a drugstore nearby that carried a few records. Treasure Island department store carried a few records. It was challenging for sure. You'd buy a few records throughout the course of a year and just play the hell out of them.

Keith: The first record I bought with my own money was *Kiss Alive* from Treasure Island. It was loud and obnoxious and your parents hated them because they looked like total freaks. Then I slowly went backwards with the first couple of Led Zeppelin records, and then Rainbow and then, like, Angel and whatever. I loved Rush. I was huge on Rush. Cheap Trick was huge. There were very few people who didn't like Cheap Trick, it seemed. They were really exciting, and their records sounded great.

Erik: You'd go down to shops like Record Head or Peaches and just kinda check stuff out. It didn't always work out; I don't think Guru Guru resonated with me quite as much as some of the other things did.

Keith: I bought a record by the Art Bears, I remember buying that and thinking it sounded like fingernails on a chalkboard.

Erik: Keith and I saw Kiss early on. I think the first concert we ever saw was the Sweet at the Riverside Theater in Milwaukee, which in retrospect was a pretty good decision on our part [laughs].

Keith: We were going to see all those bands live. Anything that came through, we'd go see. Tickets were, like, five or seven bucks, and you'd just go down and see these bands.

Like so many music fans before them, eventually the four guys started to think about playing music themselves. For Kubinski and Egeness, an interest in playing music came at a younger age, born of a general fascination with their future instruments of choice.

Dan: I knew from a very early age that I wanted to be in a band. When I was really young, I wanted to play drums.

Brian: I was five. We were driving up to my grandparents' and my grandmother said, "I have something up in the attic you might enjoy," and she came down with a violin that belonged to my great-grandmother and a mandolin from around 1894 that was my great-great-grandfather's. That's when I first became fascinated by music. I immediately started taking violin lessons. I just couldn't focus enough in class to learn the methodology and theory; I just heard the music and copied it. I was getting further along on my own by just listening to music, so I quit lessons.

Erik: I had two older cousins who played music. My cousin Chuck was playing drums, and I thought that that was really cool. My other cousin Ken was playing bass in some sort of band that I happened to see play live. I remember being mesmerized by the drummer. This kid up the street had an older brother who was kind of a hippie that played in a cover band, and I remember seeing them play "Brown Sugar" at a church picnic right around the time *Sticky Fingers* came out and just being completely mesmerized.

I remember being in grade school and waiting for fourth grade to come because that was when they gave you the option of joining the grade-school band. I wanted to play drums, and I was slightly disappointed when they gave me just a snare drum rather than a whole drum set, but I practiced a good amount.

Brian: When I was ten, my brother gave me a Blackstone guitar and amp for Christmas. And that was the start of it all. I got two Beach Boys chord books; one taught you the chords and the other taught you how to play the songs. I eventually learned all those classic Beach Boys songs. At the time, all I knew was the Beach Boys, and I'd listen to the radio and hear songs that inspired me, but for the most part nothing really hit me. I was having more fun trying to create my own music. The chord books taught me everything I needed to know. I progressed a little further and started getting into heavy rock, stuff like Zeppelin and Aerosmith and AC/DC.

Keith: I had a guitar and a little tiny amplifier that a friend of mine blew up. I tried to play guitar, and it was difficult. The first song I ever learned how to play was "Chinese Rocks" by the Heartbreakers.

Erik: That's the first thing the two of us ever played together. We didn't quite understand the lyrical content of that one at the time [laughs].

Keith: I just kind of fell into playing bass. It seemed like it would be fun to do and was a logical step for an obsessive music fan. I started playing bass simply because it seemed to be easier than playing guitar [laughs].

Brian: I had been playing guitar for a few years, and then I remember one day in 1978 that was pretty big for me. A friend of mine who was a year ahead of me told me to skip school because there was a new album out that he wanted to play for me. I got to school that morning, checked in and promptly left to go meet him across the street in the 7-Eleven parking lot. He was parked in his brown Camaro. I got in. He said, "All right, we're gonna listen to this front to back," and he put a tape in. It was Van Halen's first album. I had never heard a guitar sound like that before; it was fucking *amazing.* I got a copy of it and played it on my record player at home at 16 instead of 33 and learned "Eruption" from front to back. I couldn't play it quite as fast as he did, but in time I got there.

While Egeness and Tunison got a head start on picking up their respective instruments, Brammer's sentiment about the inaccessibility of being able to play music was something that resonated with many of his peers at the time. Regardless, music proved to be an escape for everyone. The all-too-true cliché of suburban boredom ran rampant in both cities. With little to do, teens in the '70s were left to entertain themselves.

Keith: Erik had a backyard and there was a drainage ditch, but on the edge of it we excavated it and built this sort of ice-fishing shack. It had a fireplace, and we ran electricity from his house into it so we could have a stereo in there. We'd sit out there and party. Sometimes our friends' older siblings would throw keg parties, so we'd go there and try and drink as fast as we could before the keg ran out. There were times when I'd be staggering drunk. I have no idea how my parents didn't know.

Dan: We had the Hubba Bubba factory down the street from my house, so at night we'd go there when it was closed, wait for the guard to walk by, and hop the fence. The garbage cans were filled with mis-wrapped pieces of gum, and we'd go there with pillowcases and just fill them up with gum. I think once someone got a car—we maybe went out a bit and played baseball with some mailboxes. That's what we did for fun on Friday nights.

Keith: In our group of friends, Erik and I were the only two that actually finished high school. Everyone else either dropped out or got kicked out.

There was nothing to do in the suburbs besides smoking weed and wrecking stuff. We'd go out to these warehouses and go into the dumpsters and just smash stuff and laugh. Not that I'm particularly proud of that stuff, but that's how it was. There were no entertainment options or anything. We would just sit around smoking weed and listening to music—that was it. Pretty much throughout high school I was completely stoned. If I tried smoking that much weed now, I'd probably be incapacitated! [laughs]

By the mid-1970s, rock bands were larger than life and, for superstars like David Bowie and Marc Bolan, untouchable. The barrier between performer and audience was tangible and, for a Midwestern high school kid, being on the stage was little more than a distant dream.

While Styx and Boston were playing arenas, the American underground music scene was doing something else entirely. The long, extended guitar solos, lavish stage setups, and multiple costume changes of mainstream rock were traded for concise songs with simple chord progressions that harkened back to rock 'n' roll's early days. The absence of virtuosity was, to some, hardly noticeable. The lack of traditional skills was supplemented with a raw energy and intense passion for the music. This new sector of rock 'n' roll didn't destroy the barrier between audience and performer; it simply rushed into the room screaming about how it had just discovered an unguarded entrance. Punk rock had arrived.

Erik: You always hear people talking about being the first guy in town to listen to punk rock, and in Brookfield that guy was Keith.

Keith: I used to read rock magazines voraciously. Luckily, there was a drugstore not too far down from my house that carried *Circus* and *Creem* and *Hit Parader* and *Rock Scene*. My friend Rick Carney and I got our letter printed in *Circus* once and it was pretty much your typical fifteen-year-old-

LETTERS

The editors of Circus Magazine want Letters to be an open forum for your thoughts, opinions and questions. Please send them to: Letters c/o Circus Magazine, 747 Third Avenue, New York, N. Y. 10017.

Queen's No Angel

We strongly object to the letter in Issue #157 ("Deviled Angel"). This Queen freak had no right cutting down Angel, one of the best new groups to appear on the rock scene in many years.

Anybody who hops around in a ballet costume and sings about being in love with his car and tying his mother down (Freddie Mercury) cannot be at all normal. Though Freddie has decent vocal ability and Brian suffices as an instrumentalist, we fail to see the significance of this band as a true rock form. Rock and opera mix as well as pouring Open Pit on Frosted Flakes.

If you want to hear real talent, listen to Led Zeppelin or Kiss. Jimmy Page is the best rock guitarist in the world today, and the rest of the band is equally excellent. As for Kiss, no one can match their total live energy or originality. Their music is as hard-edged rock as you will find anywhere.

The Queen is dead, long live the Kings (Zeppelin, Kiss, Angel and Aerosmith)

Rich Carney
and Keith Brammer
Brookfield, Wisconsin

P.S. The Declaration did absolutely nothing good for Anglo-American relations.

IF YOU CARE
PUNK
RECORD GUIDE
NUGENT • McCARTNEY • FOGHAT • ABBA • RAMONES
02137
APRIL 1978 $1.00
America's Only Rock 'n' Roll Magazine
CREEM
QUEEN
Back To Basics
Champs Or Chumps?
EXCLUSIVE!
Candid Conversation With
ERIC CLAPTON
Racism, Money, Love and Glory
NASHVILLE BABYLON!
ELVIS
The Pharaoh of Tupelo
ROCK FILM FEST:
THE WHO's The Kids Are
DYLAN's Renaldo & Clara
PATTI SMITH's Junkey
FERNWOOD'S MU
Turns The Other Che
WAYLON & WIL
Cowboy Chic
WET WILLIE
Sink Or Swim?
ANGEL • STAR
ROCKETS • TU
JAM • TUFF D
CROCK AWA
Is Punk Dead
SEX PISTOLS
Invade & Fad
CHAOS
SUPER PUNK
JOHNNY
ROTTEN
Spits Out The Truth!
0 71486 02137 04

with-an-attitude sort of thing. The point of the letter was that we thought Queen sucked and Aerosmith was awesome, or something to that effect.

Hit Parader was one of the first magazines that would write about stuff like the Ramones and the Dictators. I remember reading about the Ramones and thinking that it sounded like something I'd really like. Finding the record in Brookfield wasn't happening for me, though. Somehow my mom was able to order a copy of it from somewhere and gave it to me for Christmas that year. She instantly regretted it [laughs].

Dan: It was 1976 and I remember watching something on TV about the Queen's Jubilee, and I remember hearing the news anchor say something about the Sex Pistols, and there they were, looking all dirty and fucked up. It just seemed really odd to me at the time. It wasn't until '77 or '78 when I got that issue of *Creem* with Johnny Rotten on the cover. I went to my favorite department store and saw *Never Mind the Bollocks* in the rack. I took that along with Heart's *Little Queen* stuffed them under my jacket and walked right out the door.

Brian: I ran into this friend of mine named Lou Name, and he said to me, "You gotta hear this new music." I went over to his house, and he played me the first Sex Pistols album, and that was it—it was so fucking cool. He gave me some European music magazine that I can't recall the name of, but it just had a list of all these U.K. punk bands, and one of them was Wire. I really liked the dissonance, energy, and the emotion behind it, and that's what I gravitated towards. I don't really care much for technique. If you've got soul behind what you're trying to play, what more do you need?

Keith: There was a record store called Peaches around here where I was able to find imports. I'd go there and get the first Clash record on import, a Thin Lizzy record, and some other art-rock thing or whatever. That was the whole genesis of the thing I was reading about; you'd find out about these bands by reading about them.

Ian MacKaye (member, Minor Threat; co-founder, Dischord Records): The punk clarion was the call for self-definition. You could do whatever you want—you just designed your own life. You could get punk records, like the stuff coming out of England or the West Coast, and obviously the Ramones records. If you're a kid in America, there was no moving visual information for you—all you had was the records and maybe a few magazines here and there. Fanzines still hadn't really existed yet. What the artists were doing, it was left for you to figure it out.

While Tunison affectionately points to Brammer as being one of Brookfield's earliest fans of punk rock, the scene in Rockford was very much centered around a guy by the name of Don Busch, affectionately known amongst his peers as "Toothpaste."

Dan: I knew this guy we called Toothpaste. He traveled to Germany once or twice and brought back a lot of punk rock records in 1978. He brought back a couple of Saints LPs that we hadn't heard yet and the second Wire record that we didn't even know existed. That first Eddie and the Hotrods record, *Teenage Depression,* was pretty big with my group of friends. The Dead Boys, too.

Brian "Beezer" Hill (bassist, the Stellas): Toothpaste was *the* punk rocker at Gilford High. The first time I ever heard Wire was through him. He had the *Pink Flag* LP. He had all kinds of stuff I had never heard before like *Raw Power* and the New York Dolls records. But yeah, the whole scene revolved around Toothpaste. His mom worked second shift, so when she left he'd open his house to whoever wanted to come over. It was a budding bunch of punk rock kids at our school, and Dan was one of them.

Dan: A lot of that late-'60s and early-'70s stuff I heard through Toothpaste. By the time I was sixteen or seventeen, most of the records I bought came from the cutout bin, stuff like Iggy Pop and Bowie and Sparks.

Brad Wood (producer, Liz Phair, Smashing Pumpkins, Placebo): I was aware of Dan because I went to Guilford High. Dan must've been a junior when I was a freshman or something. He was an intimidatingly cool presence there. He was aggressively punk rock and very open about his love of things like Bowie—and that was in those Berlin years! He dressed well—he had cool hair. I think I remember him catching hell from the principal at the time just for looking the way he did, and that principal was a stereotypical dick. I remember him hanging around people who were way cooler than anyone I knew, and I never had the courage to even say a word to him.

[Toothpaste] was a huge part of that scene for sure. I knew his younger sister Renatta, and she was at least as cool as he was. Those people were on the pointy end of the punk rock sphere, and they paid the price for it because they were ostracized for their interests. I was never brave enough at that age to publicly claim that I was into anything that was punk rock or new wave. I didn't have the stones for that as a freshman.

Keith: I remember having my dad use a Telex machine to get me a copy of *Raw Power* from the U.K. It was basically a precursor to the fax machine, but all the messages came through in print.

Erik: You used to see them on the old *Mission: Impossible* show at the beginning of each episode!

Keith: He knew these people, and he got them to send over a copy of *Raw Power.* I still remember it saying "pay no more than £1.99" on it.

A lot of those records were all out of print by the time we heard about them. They came out and were gone, unless you could find a used copy of them somewhere. I remember reading about *Metallic K.O.* and sending away for that from the back of *Rock Scene* or something. It meant so much more when you read about it and built it up in your head and then you finally found it. And then it just felt like it was yours—you stuck with it.

Everyone I was hanging around with was listening to all this sort of stuff, really. But at the same time, we were hearing other things. There was one summer where it seemed like everywhere you went they were playing Pink Floyd's *Animals.* Thankfully, none of us were listening to REO Speedwagon or Kansas or whatever.

While the four kids had yet to meet, they were all on a similar path of discovering new music. Some of them took to the genre a little later, however.

Keith: Erik was a little more selective in his tastes. It took him a little while before he started to really get into some of the punk rock stuff we were listening to.

Erik: Punk didn't connect with me right away. It wasn't really a huge connection for me until later. Hearing those first few American hardcore records is what really got me into it, and then it really fell into place, and that got me to go back and listen to the Ramones and the Clash.

What did make an impact on me was seeing the Talking Heads on *Saturday Night Live.* [February 10, 1979]. I went out the very next day and bought *More Songs about Buildings and Food.* That really spoke to me.

Inspired by the raw and honest qualities of the bands that they loved, it was just a matter of time before the four friends decided to make music of their own. The Clash and Patti Smith famously encouraged their audiences to start their own bands, which was delivered more as a mandate rather than a suggestion.

Punk was still a relatively new phenomenon, and finding like-minded individuals proved to be challenging in both Rockford and Brookfield. Similarly-minded people often tend to gravitate towards one another, though, and over time fans of punk rock slowly began to find one another.

Keith: I'd read all these editorials in *Flipside* or whatever and see people saying things like, "Yeah, there's only like twenty punks at our school," and I'd just laugh and be like, "Twenty isn't enough? We've got two!" There just weren't that many people who were into it from around here.

Brian "Beezer" Hill (bassist, The Stellas): Right as my peer group and I were coming into our own in Milwaukee, I was uprooted and taken to Rockford. When I got there, I was blown away by the absolute nothingness of the place. There wasn't anything going on. The downtown area at the time was all one-way streets that all went around this mall section. No one ever went downtown. The business district had nothing going on.

I think I bought the Sex Pistols' "God Save the Queen" single, like, the week I moved there and loved it. I thought I was the only person in the world that was going to listen to this kind of music. When I started school and saw a bunch of people who already were into that, it was kind of eye-opening. And all those people became my new peer group in Rockford.

Things happened gradually in the pre-internet era. Information was spread via fanzines, buying physical records, and seeing bands live. The seed of starting a band had been planted, but the idea felt more out of reach when there wasn't a blueprint to follow or a local community to join. Slowly, the respective scenes in Rockford and Milwaukee began to develop and, with that, so did the desire to finally start a band.

Keith: All those experiences of doing nothing really informed the whole punk rock thing. It was like when we finally got around to it it was such a release after all these years of just absolutely nothing happening.

Brian: I was going to Rockford East High, and Dan came to a dance there. Lou and I were there, and we ran into him just kinda like, ". . . punk rock, huh? Okay, cool." We got to talking and eventually started to play music together.

Dan: Brian Egeness and I had been playing in an all-covers punk rock band called the Stains. I think we put on a handful of shows, nothing major. I think we played a house party, and I sang with my back to the audience the whole time.

Erik: The bands I played in early on weren't that serious. A couple of gigs here and there and we'd last for a few months. It was good and informative; they were into writing songs which I immediately gravitated towards. It helped me figure out how being in a band worked. It was a really good learning experience.

Keith: I've said it so many times, but the Ramones made a huge impression on me in terms of actually playing music. Kiss made me want to be in a band, but the Ramones convinced me that I *could* be in a band. A lot of people have said the same thing, but they really convinced me that anyone could do this. It wasn't rocket science, and you didn't have to be Chris Squier from Yes.

Dan: Lou Name played bass and was all about putting a band together, so he and I got together with Brian on guitar and this other guy Grant on drums. It wasn't too long afterwards that our friend Beezer came into the picture. He came over one day and asked if we wanted to start playing together. He had the idea of calling the band the Stellas. When he joined on bass, Lou switched to guitar, so we had two guitarists.

Beezer: I was playing with the Ciaccio brothers in a band called the Stellas. The name came from this painting that one of the dudes got at a thrift store of this homely girl with a super-long neck. It was strange, and for some reason we always called that painting Stella. They eventually changed their name to the Tense Experts, and when I started playing with Dan and Brian Egeness we just decided to use the old name for our new band.

The Stellas' Rockford lineup existed for a short span of time, with Dan Kubinski on vocals, Brian "Beezer" Hill on bass, Brian Egeness on guitar, and Grant Pierce on drums. Musically, they were drawing on first-wave '70s punk—things like the Sex Pistols, the Clash, Wire, 999, and the Dickies. The group never officially recorded, but a soundboard recording from one of their gigs shows signs of what the future sound could be. Slower, less frantic, and more tuneful, the Stellas were a simple but solid punk band,

The first phase of the Stellas as they play live in Rockford, Illinois, c. 1981. Courtesy of the Die Kreuzen. Photographer unknown.

with a heavy influence from the more melody-heavy side of late-'70s punk. Plenty of covers by 999, Dead Kennedys, and the Germs were a part of the band's repertoire, as well as a small handful of originals that eventually became Die Kreuzen songs. Tracks like "Mannequin" and "Hate Me" are dramatically slower than the Die Kreuzen versions, sounding closer to Dangerhouse Records seven-inches than Bad Brains. Though never officially released, one can hear the beginnings of the band forming their own sound on these recordings. Hill's bass playing is punchy, Egeness's guitar playing is confident, and, even this early on, it's apparent that Kubinski is aiming for a more aggressive vocal approach than other vocalists at the time.

As for many adolescents growing up at the time, anywhere seemed better than Rockford to the young musicians, so a plan was hatched to leave home and relocate to Milwaukee.

Beezer: We all lived together at that time, and we all looked at each other one night and realized that we were all working terrible jobs and that we'd be better off leaving for Milwaukee. Brian and I were working at Rockford College in the cafeteria. I remember one day that we decided we were just going to leave at lunchtime and never look back.

There was this guy named Paul who was our roadie—he hung around with all of us. He and some of the guys were hanging out in the parking lot at the high school during a powderpuff football game. There was this car with a sunroof, and the sunroof was open, and the keys were in the ignition. One of them just jumped into the car from the sunroof, unlocked the car, started it and drove it to my house.

They showed up on my doorstep and said, "Don't ask any questions, but we're leaving for Milwaukee right now." I said, "Okay, cool", threw whatever I had in my dresser in a bag, and took off. It didn't matter to me if I spent another ten minutes in Rockford. I was way done with the place.

Brian: The car was in the Gilford High parking lot. We climbed in through the sunroof, took the car, parked it behind a church, and went home to tell our parents that we were moving. We went and picked up the car, got on the highway, and started driving. About halfway up to Milwaukee, the car died. We were trying to figure out what to do, so we ended up putting all the stuff we had in my car and driving the rest of the way.

We drove it to a gas station and paid to have it repaired, parked it in a cornfield, put the keys back in the woman's purse, and then someone called her and gave her directions on how to find the car. We didn't take any money from her or anything like that.

Dan: We got this show in Milwaukee opening up for the Tense Experts, who were friends of ours from Rockford that had recently moved up there. We had a blast playing that show, and I think about a week later Brian and Beezer had decided that they were going to move up there. I dropped out of school and headed up there with them.

Keith: I think it was around 1980. The Stellas had been coming up to Milwaukee from Rockford and I immediately was into what they were doing. Most of the bands around here were doing a super pop new wave sort of thing, or else they were arty. I was hanging out with the Tense Experts at their place on Brady Street, and through them I started hanging around the Stellas guys.

With a new home base and the excitement of being there, the Stellas were set to move forward as a band. There was just one problem: Grant had decided to stay back in Rockford, leaving the Stellas without a drummer. A new headquarters had been secured; the next order of business was to find a new drummer.

Beezer: We moved in with the Tense Experts, who had moved up there. They were living at this house on 27th and State. We started immediately auditioning drummers.

Keith: I moved down to the East Side and started hanging out with the Stellas guys. I was hanging around them and doing "lights" at their live shows, which meant that I flipped things on and off. It didn't matter because I just wanted to be around. Eventually, I came to find out that they had been going through a ton of drummers and were looking for someone to play for them. I suggested Erik to them and told them to give him a call.

Brian: We had seen a band that Keith was in at Zak's. We got to talking with him, and he was a fantastic bass player, and he said he knew of a drummer that was looking to play in a band. That turned out to be Erik.

Erik: It was a case of Keith introducing me to Dan, Brian, and Beezer because they needed a drummer.

Beezer: It was just like suddenly Erik appeared in a room and introduced himself to us. We tried him out and gelled well with him. I wasn't even sure if he was into punk rock at the time, but he played so well with us that it didn't even really matter.

Erik: Meeting them just immediately changed everything for me. Just like, "Wow, here's something that's really happening." I met them and instantly it was, "Okay, here we go."

Richard Kohl (visual artist, manager, Die Kreuzen): I remember seeing them in Chicago with the Effigies. That was a very eventful show—they were always pretty good about practicing, but they had gotten better. O'Banion's was a fun place to play, but it was kind of a dump and there was no stage and the crowd was pretty nutty. I remember this super-tall skinhead chick shoved the mic in Danny's mouth—like, hard. It was rough. Even with all that, they still played a great set, I recall.

Erik: That thirty-minute set at O'Banion's completely made our reputation in Chicago. From then on we always did pretty well there.

A great gig in a tough market and personnel change were setting the Stellas on the path to success. With Tunison behind the drum kit, the band started to realize that they needed to upgrade the other half of their rhythm section as well, replacing Beezer Hill with Keith Brammer on bass.

Erik: It was a few months before we decided to get Keith to join. I was thrilled to have my buddy Keith in the band.

Dan: After getting Erik in the band, we decided that we wanted to take the band more seriously—practice more and play more shows and record and all that kind of stuff. We started to realize that Keith was probably a better fit for us as a bass player than Beezer.

Keith: I remember riding with them down to that gig at O'Banion's, and we went out to eat before the show. At that point, Beezer was a solid bass player. He was arguably a better bassist than I was, because he was very melodic in his playing. But they sat me down and kinda explained the situation to me and asked if I would be interested in playing bass for them, and I of course said yes. That was it.

This new change, of course, wasn't as easy as asking Keith to join. Beezer was still in the band, and he had to be informed of their decision to replace him with Keith.

Dan: When it came to letting Beezer know that he wasn't gonna be playing with us anymore, we didn't handle that situation very well. Plus, we were all working together at Pizza Man at the time, so it was awkward for a little while there between us.

Beezer: It was definitely weird. We had a sit-down at Pizza Man and I remember saying, "If we can work this out . . ." and they were just all like, "Nah, we can't." By that point, they had decided that they were going to have Keith join the band. In that regard, it was mutual in a way.

The most uncomfortable part about it was that we still had to work together and see each other every day. We had come so far together in a sense, moving to Milwaukee for the sake of the band.

Dan: Beezer formed a new band called Sacred Order within a few weeks of that happening, though. So that was cool.

Change was happening quickly, not only for the Stellas but for punk rock as well. By 1981, punk's first wave faded, got scrubbed clean, and was repackaged as new wave. Music videos by new wave artists started to pop up on a then-brand-new cable channel called MTV, and the sound that was once underground had now mutated into some of the most popular music in the world. People who loved the punk of the '70s felt different, though, as the sound was viewed as a removal of punk's best qualities, slicked up for the purpose of mainstream consumption. In the eyes of the mainstream, punk was dead.

To the underground, the sound of punk had been co-opted by new wave, and the need to move things forward presented itself. As a result, a new breed of bands started to appear in the underground. The difference between them was clear—songs were shorter and faster, replacing melody with an amped-up aggression. Plenty of terms were thrown around to describe this newer and more unhinged younger sibling of punk—thrash and speed—but none of them stuck around for very long. Thanks to Vancouver's DOA and their landmark album *Hardcore 81*, the genre had found its identity. It wasn't just punk anymore; it was hardcore punk.

Erik: At the time we thought what we were doing was pretty fast, but compared to what we'd do later it was definitely more on the midtempo side of things.

Brian: All of a sudden, we started hearing the early Black Flag singles and the Dead Kennedys records, and we thought that those bands had more of an edge than the earlier English stuff that we'd been listening to. All these new bands just exploded onto the scene, and we started seeing and meeting them. It was a natural progression for us to start writing songs with a similar sort of edge.

Punk rock bands started to form in Southern California, taking the Ramones blueprint to places it had yet to go. Bands started to pop up in Los Angeles and the surrounding areas, often with an emphasis on ramshackle aggression. Among the lot, the Germs and Circle Jerks were two acts responsible for pushing the genre forward and influence legions of others in their wake.

Keith: *GI* by the Germs was just huge for all of us at that time. That and *Group Sex* by the Circle Jerks were just mind-blowing. We knew it was something different. At the time we thought the Circle Jerks were the fastest thing we ever heard. We'd just listen to and marvel at the speed of those songs.

Brian: We just liked the energy. We just started playing the songs faster and faster. We rehearsed a lot, just trying to get them faster.

Keith: It was more like, "Let's see what we can do with this."

Erik: I think we just kinda decided, "Well, if we're gonna do this, we may as well do it the best we can and not only be fast, but be *tight*."

Thurston Moore (vocals, guitar, Sonic Youth): A lot of bands were just informing each other about speed. They were getting information by seeing bands from D.C., which was really potent for bands in Detroit and Ann Arbor. The idea of playing faster was just kind of a way of becoming newer and more connected to each other. It was this shared idea of speed.

Dan: I didn't like the sound of my voice when I sang, and so I think I just wanted to screw it up a little bit and disguise it. My favorite singers, in no particular order, are Darby Crash, Steven Tyler, John Lydon—all these guys who sing kind of monotone and gravelly. I heard this alternate version of "Anarchy in the U.K." where John was singing with a lot more power than what ended up being the version on the album. It was so snotty and harsh.

Over a few months in 1981, the Stellas' sound evolved into something new. The increased tempos and energy, the more aggressive vocal approach,

and, now, a brand-new member all came together to further develop their sound.

Keith: I remember learning all the songs in about three days because we had a show at the Palms. I'd get to their apartment after they had gotten out of work at 2 a.m. and just practice on these tiny practice amps in their living room. We'd go until 7 a.m. and then just pass out.

Beezer: They changed dramatically after I left. I remember seeing them open for X not long after we had stopped playing together, and everything was like two to three times faster than how we had been playing them just a few months previously. They had really become a fast hardcore band, and that really wasn't my thing. I was way more into the way the Pistols and the Clash played.

Erik: I think the idea was that we were clearly a different outfit at that point. We wanted to clear the air and make a new definitive thing.

Brian: We changed our name in October of 1981. We were kind of a fuckabout band early on, so we wanted to establish ourselves as something different from the Stellas—something a little more focused and serious.

Keith: Our friend Diane Strand came up with the name, actually. She found it in a book, and she decided that she was going to start a band and call it Die Kreuzen. When we decided that we were going to change our name, we literally stole it from her [laughs]. We all knew she was never gonna actually start a band.

Dan: It just looked cool on paper. At the time we didn't even know what it meant.

***Kreuzen* is a German word which is the plural form of cross. Add the leading article of Die and the name becomes the Crosses. Visually, Die Kreuzen looked and sounded like no other band names in Milwaukee at the time—fittingly so, as the band was making music very much out of step with most of their peers—a distinct-sounding name for a distinct-sounding band. It looked great, sounded great when pronounced correctly, and helped them establish themselves as a band to be taken seriously.** ●

The band in a very early promotional photo, captured in their natural Midwestern winter habitat. Photo: Richard Kohl.

Early photos of Die Kreuzen live onstage at the Palms in Milwaukee, c. 1982. Photo: Murray Kappel / Jennifer Leazer

Becoming Die Kreuzen

A NEW NAME AND LINEUP CAN DO A LOT FOR A BAND, and in the case of Die Kreuzen it was transformative. A new bass player. A new name. With the final lineup of Tunison on drums, Kubinski on vocals, Egeness on guitar, and now Brammer on bass, everything fell into place. The band was ready to get to work.

In 1982, though, punk was seen as past its sell-by date. New wave had found its way into the mainstream in a major way, and the public's enthusiasm for it was just as present in Milwaukee. Milwaukee's punk scene was small, with fluid boundaries, as musicians and fans bounced between punk, new wave, and all sub-sub-genres in between. Die Kreuzen's take on hardcore punk earned them impressive local opener spots for the touring punk and hardcore bands. They shared bills with Black Flag, X, Bad Brains, Circle Jerks, TSOL, and Flipper and numerous other bands hopping in the van during this era of DIY tours.

Keith: We were the red-headed stepchild of the Milwaukee music scene at that time. Milwaukee was much more supportive of out-of-town acts than it was of any of the bands that lived there. People treated punk rock as passé, as though they were so far beyond it by that point.

Erik: We were really the only band in town that played this kind of music, so we were very fortunate that we got asked to be the opener for a lot of the cooler out-of-town acts who came through town.

Kenny Baldwin owned the Starship and played drums in many Milwaukee bands. His club was one of the first to host "punk" and non-mainstream bands, booking everyone from Wendy O. Williams and the Plasmatics to the Sun-Ra Arkestra. Photo: Kevin Hutchison.

Being one of the city's few punk rock acts at the time certainly worked to their advantage, but opportunities rarely find the person; rather, they are given to them by someone else. For Die Kreuzen, many of their early opening slots were thanks to the help of a local club owner named Kenny Baldwin who booked shows at a venue called the Starship.

Baldwin died at age sixty-two in 2015 of lung cancer. He was a beloved figure on the Milwaukee music scene and his impact was, and still is, immeasurable, as he had a gift for spotting talented bands.

Keith: Kenny Baldwin was immensely important to the Milwaukee music scene at the time, because there really was no place else to play. The Starship was literally the only game in town; there were no other clubs.

Dan: We played the Starship on a Saturday night as the Stellas. He was super-nice and told us to come back any time. Kenny was like a father figure to me; he was a little bit older and an accomplished drummer. Kenny taught us how to conduct ourselves at a venue; how to be kind and gracious and not just show up at a gig and be disrespectful to the venue. Be friendly to the sound guy because they're gonna make you sound good. You're gonna be here for the next five or six hours around these people—may as well make it comfortable for everyone.

Erik: We were lucky to have Kenny Baldwin's support, because he would give us the opening slots for all the great shows. Black Flag, TSOL, X—we played all those shows because of Kenny.

Keith: He was at least about a decade older than us and had inherited this club that used to be a strip joint. He wanted to do something with it, at that point it was more of a disco kinda thing. Jerome, who played in this band called the Haskels, he was the one who hipped Kenny to the local punk rock bands. He just didn't discriminate; anyone could play there.

Dan: The Starship was a music-focused bar first and foremost. Sure, the punk and new wave thing was what was happening at the time but, if you look at some of the shows they had there, there were definitely plenty of shows that weren't like that. That was because of Kenny. I remember seeing that the Ventures were playing there a little later, probably around '85?

Keith: He was one of us. Sure, there were rules that you had to follow: don't break things or whatever, and we could respect that. It was more like a clubhouse for us than it was a club, because we lived right down the street for a while. We didn't care who was playing, we'd just go there and prop up the bar and drink.

I remember Kenny would always be like, "All right, I'm buying shots," and you knew what it was gonna be—it was gonna be ginger brandy. That stuff—wow; it was like drinking paint thinner.

Erik: I think that ginger brandy he probably inherited from two or three previous owners of the club.

Keith: Most of the time Kenny would let us in for free just because he knew we'd spend every cent we had at the bar. We'd hang out after everyone had gone home.

Erik: My first gig with them [Die Kreuzen] was the first Black Flag show at the Starship when we were still called the Stellas. Dez [Cadena] was singing for them and Henry [Rollins] was hanging with the band. That was a really wild introduction. They were in a completely different league. They showed up with two trucks and a bunch of stage equipment and just took over—that's what I remember. It was really eye-opening to see these guys come from out of town and just take over. It felt really inspiring—just like, "Wow, this is so cool!"

Dan: We played with Bad Brains at the Starship. They were really late to the show, I recall. We played our set, and the place was packed, and everyone was just kind of waiting around. They showed up, loaded on stage, and started playing. Their roadie had the biggest joint in the world and started passing it around to the band members—while they were playing! And they didn't miss a note, man. They were totally next level in terms of performance, just amazing to watch. Of course, the place started filling up with smoke and Kenny freaked [laughs].

Richard Kohl: The only two established places were Zak's and the Starship, and they played both of them a ton. That place got so trashed after the Circle Jerks, and these little kids came out of the woodwork, never seen these people before, and they just came out like ants. Beer spilled everywhere, tables broken and turned over—these kids were ripping the horns out of the PA speakers. I took a stick and I poked around these tables not sure of what I was gonna find—it was really like a battle zone.

Like many rust-belt cities during the eighties, downtown Milwaukee was a wasteland of buildings emptied during the Reagan recession. Much as in New York and Los Angeles, downtown Milwaukee had its fair share of cheap apartments. The Norman was the Chelsea Hotel of Milwaukee, home to musicians, artists, wannabes, and other margin walkers. This was perfect for four young musicians looking to further integrate themselves into the scene.

Richard Kohl: Me and my friend Angie and this other girl Kelly moved into Norman. The Ama-Dots had found the apartment building. At night it was so dead, and the rent was so incredibly cheap. We all decided to just move in together at the same time. I think between the three of us rent was maybe like $200 total.

The tenants previous to us were Outlaw motorcycle guys. There wasn't any evidence of that besides the fact they had painted everything dark brown. Someone had taken a shotgun and shot up one of the closets, and it was such a mess, and the building manager wouldn't fix it. A lot of people came in and out of there. A lot of people lived there. This girl Diane Strand moved into this one bedroom on our floor, and at one point she invited Die Kreuzen to live with her, sleeping on the sofas and whatnot.

Above: The early days of Die Kreuzen at the Norman Apartments in 1982. From left to right: Brian Egeness, Keith Brammer, Dan Kubinski, and Erik Tunison.

Below: Brian poses in the kitchen of the band's apartment at the Norman in 1982. Photos: Richard Kohl.

The man, the myth, the legend—visual artist and one-time Die Kreuzen manager Richard Kohl. Photo: Richard Kohl.

Keith: It was like musical chairs at the Norman because there were many cheap apartments. When Diane moved out, I got the bedroom and Dan slept in the closet. I think we were paying like $175 a month in total for that place. The ones on the end were three bedrooms—those were like $220 or something. We had nothing to speak of, really. I think we had a hotplate and an electric frying pan.

Dan: We had a little black and white TV that I had since I was a kid. The one thing we did have was a decent stereo system. We built some sort of Frankenstein stereo system where we played our records and cassettes. Erik was staying there a lot by then.

Erik: It played a really big role in a lot of things, not only music but art as well. It really was the Chelsea Hotel of Milwaukee. There were tons of artists, photographers, transients, and old folks living there. We were able to get away with almost everything, and it was walking distance from the Starship. The rent was low, and some apartments had enough space for half a dozen people to each have their own room. It was great.

Brian: It was a party atmosphere, but more than anything I just sat and played guitar a lot. It helped me work out a lot of shit when I was younger, so I just buried myself in that. We all had the same goal, so living, working, and playing together wasn't an issue.

Dan: We lived there for pretty much the entirety of the existence of the Starship, which was convenient because the Norman was like two blocks down the street. There were times when we'd literally be pushing our amps down the street from the Norman to the Starship.

Keith: I remember we used to play at the Starship and invite a few people to come over after the show, and we'd get there and there'd be like 100 people hanging out.

Dan: The apartment manager, John, was this big muscular dude who lived down the hall and up a floor. We'd be outside on the balcony drinking beers thinking we were being really quiet and all of a sudden you'd just notice him standing there for who knows how long, just completely silent. He didn't have to say anything at all.

Keith: We'd go and kick out everyone or pretend to kick out everyone but really just kick out the people we didn't want there to begin with.

Richard Kohl: That was when they started bugging me about managing them. I think other people were telling them to use me as their manager, and I also was getting some support from people I knew telling me to do it. I was on the fence about it for a while. My big question was "why me?" I couldn't figure it out.

I was also sporadically putting out a fanzine—I believe it was something we'd revamp and change the title on. The first issue interviewed them, and I think that kinda cemented it. Shortly after, I was managing them, and there weren't really a lot of specifics besides to get them more shows.

Things were so transitory back then. I figured I had just dropped out of school—I was working full time in a factory silk-screening yardsticks. The one thing that made me decide to do it was that they were so determined about it. That kind always threw me off about them because you didn't see that in a lot of people their age at the time. I figured, "Well, okay, why not?" I had no experience as a manager, and I'm sure I told them that. I don't remember, but it happened.

New Year's Eve 1981 was the very first night that I managed them. They were playing at the Starship. The Oil Tasters played upstairs, and Kenny had us playing downstairs. We were just hanging out drinking beers or whatever, and my friend looks at me and says, "What's that in your beer?" I look in the glass and just see that there's a hit of blotter acid in there. And I thought, "Great, this is the first night managing them, and I don't even know what to do," I ask Brian what he needs me to do, and he takes me back behind the mixing board and says, "You see these meters here? Just make sure all these arrows are all pointing in the red, just as far as you can go." The music was really, really fucking loud, the ceiling is super-low, so it starts getting really claustrophobic.

I'm standing back there, pretty nervous, and then off to the side I see this really nice disco-looking couple come in. He's got this nice white leisure suit on, and she's all dolled up, and the rest of the people are in, like, denim and black leather jackets and boots. This couple goes right out into the middle of the dance floor where everyone is slam-dancing, and then this girl started messing with the girl who was dancing, and then her boyfriend went after her, and then elbows started getting thrown and then the next thing you know it, the whole place just erupted. All these people from all four corners of the room just in this massive monkey pile. I saw the instruments go down and even the guys in the band were out there.

And there I was watching it all happen, tripping on acid. Oh, good lord.

Being a stone's throw away from the Starship ensured not only that the band often could be found hanging out at the venue but that they could also put up touring bands who needed a place to stay after the show.

Thurston Moore: I knew about the Stellas because you'd read about them in all those scene reports at the time, and then it seemed like they quickly changed their name to Die Kreuzen. I remember talking to Henry Rollins

Four friends putzing around in a photo booth, c. 1982.
Photo courtesy of Die Kreuzen.

about them back in the '80s and him talking about how Black Flag stayed with them. It seemed like they just had this reputation of being this awesome Milwaukee hardcore band that everyone would hang out with when they came through town.

Keith: I remember when the Misfits were scheduled to play at the Starship, and it was pretty early on so no one really knew who they were or really cared about them. When they got into town on the day of the show there was this gigantic snowstorm—like, all of downtown Milwaukee was completely shut down. There must have been three feet of snow there, so, needless to say, the show got shut down.

Erik: Ray Morris from Six Feet Under in Chicago put them in touch with us. They gave us a call asking if they could crash with us. Lucky for them our phone didn't get shut off that week.

Brian: Kenny didn't think that anyone was gonna show up because of the snow, so he canceled the show.

Keith: We were all just at our apartment and we just hear this huge knock at the door. We open the door and there's the Misfits, these super-tall dudes and then this shorter guy. Doyle and Jerry Only were both, like, well over six feet tall. I open the door and I'm like, "Holy shit," just looking at these super-tall dudes. Jerry was holding the bass guitar with the skull on the headstock, no case, just standing there with it, completely covered in snow.

Erik: In full Misfits regalia! Leather jackets, devilocks—exactly as you'd expect them to be, standing outside of our door

Keith: We put them up for the night, and they were perfectly affable guys. Glenn Danzig and Brian were like two peas in a pod, I remember. They were talking about coffins and books and all kinds of stuff.

Brian: I remember taking Glenn Danzig down to a comic book store because he was looking for some Barbarella comics. He was definitely nice enough at the time.

Keith: They were like, "Oh we're gonna kick that Kenny guy's ass," and we were like, "Nah, mellow out, he's a good guy, there's no power here, dudes." No one was gonna come to the show, 'cause, like, remember, this was still really early on. No one really knew who they were yet. That's how it was back then—you may have been big in Chicago or Detroit, but in Milwaukee you were exactly no one.

Erik: They also laid a bunch of merch on us, which subsequently is now worth thousands of dollars [laughs].

Keith: Huge stacks of the first pressing of the *Walk among Us* record. Tons of posters that would probably fetch hundreds of dollars each now. And we gave them all away to our friends [laughs].

The band was slowly building its reputation on the regional and national circuit while the members were refining their sound and developing their performance skills. Going to a professional studio was out of the question and not within their budget, so for their earliest recordings they called on the services of a friend who owned a four-track reel-to-reel machine.

Keith: We recorded at Bill Stace's apartment on Murray Avenue. He had a back cottage with a studio in the basement. It was pretty bare-bones.

Bill Stace (recording engineer, drummer, Ama-Dots): I recorded their demos on a Teac quarter-inch reel-to-reel four-track recorder. I had some AKG mics, some little six-channel Tapco mixer—just a mishmash of stuff that I could put together. It was all really stripped down. I had really minimal equipment at that time.

We pretty much did it all live, I was just sitting in the room with them while they ran through the songs. It couldn't have been more than a couple of days, really. It was probably mixed on headphones, honestly. That's all we were really able to do back then!

Dan: The first demo cassette came not long after that. My girlfriend at the time was an aspiring graphic designer, and she had made this piece with a bunch of crosses on it, and I liked that, so I shrunk it down to where it would fit as a cassette insert and used a typeset that I got from Richard Kohl. We dubbed them to those really cheap Tonemaster cassettes that you could get in packs of three for a dollar, just like the worst cassettes you could possibly buy.

Erik: We bought the best cassettes that we could afford, which were still terrible quality, and just dubbed them with two cassette decks.

Had Die Kreuzen suffered the fate of many young bands by breaking up far too soon, this demo would have been the source of so many what-ifs. This nine-song collection shows a band that truly cared about their craft. It's an accurate document of their repertoire at the time—short and fast hardcore

The band recording gang vocals, likely for "All White," c. 1982. Photo courtesy of Die Kreuzen.

punk songs that sat well alongside fellow Midwestern acts like Negative Approach, the Fix, and Mecht Mensch. The basic structures of the songs are there, and there are slight differences between these versions and ones that appeared on later releases. Egeness's guitar solo for "In School" features a quick and subtle nod to "Ring around the Rosie." "No Name" features a loose vocal arrangement from Kubinski, who was coming into his own as a singer. Songs like "Pain" and "Hate Me" are delivered at nearly double the tempo as the Stellas versions, but the band does so without losing their grip on the arrangements. True to their word, they ramped up the tempos while still maintaining a tight precision to the performances.

Using the network of hardcore fanzines at the time, the band was able to get their home-made cassettes into the hands of anyone who sent them cash through the mail. The widespread underground network of hardcore punk ensured that these cassettes would travel far outside of the Midwest.

Lou Barlow (member, Deep Wound, Dinosaur Jr., Sebadoh): I have this old notebook where I'd write down stuff that I wanted to buy or track down or whatever. I have Die Kreuzen in there, but I have it written down as "Die Cruisin," which is hilarious. I must have wanted to check them out after hearing them on the *Charred Remains* compilation, because J [Mascis] had that.

I ended up ordering that demo cassette from a 'zine. It was this homemade cassette that I got in the mail. I still have it! The labels fell off 'cause it's so old. The music was all really emotional and purposeful. It was more psychological and mysterious. The name was mysterious. I just loved that demo so much.

Even then, that band was *tight*. They could obviously play—that was a huge part of it. The guitar playing was super-interesting, the vocals were badass. It was just clear right away that they could play really well, like on the same level as the Dead Kennedys or Bad Brains. That was never a prerequisite, and I love completely inept and sloppy sounding records, but there weren't a whole lot of hardcore bands that you could hear and immediately think, "Oh my god, all these guys can really play."

Kim Thayil (guitarist, Soundgarden): Between 1982 and 1984, I was working at a college radio station called KCMU, which is now KEXP. I did a cover story for the radio newsletter where I interviewed Mark Arm's band at the time, Mr. Epp and the Calculations. I asked them to name the fastest punk rock bands they could think of. They were just throwing out names, but if

A high-energy Die Kreuzen live gig, with no barrier between the band and their audience, c. 1983. Photo: Kevin Hutchison.

I recall, their answers included Void, the Meatmen, Minor Threat, and Die Kreuzen. It was overwhelming, because there was so much music happening at the time, but at that point I knew of Die Kreuzen for their speed.

Kubinski's lyrics drew more on the personal than on the political. Many punk and hardcore bands at the time chose to focus their anger on President Reagan, often to the point of cliché. Rarely ones to follow the flock, Die Kreuzen made the conscious choice of avoiding political statements.

Dan: My grandparents used to fight a lot at the kitchen table. My grandmother was a Republican and used to complain about my grandfather, the "goddamn Democrat." I was always told that it wasn't polite to discuss religion or politics at the dinner table. I guess I grew up that way and didn't really think about it until I became old enough to vote and understood the power of all that.

There were so many bands whose lyrics addressed the political climate at the time. I didn't want to be matter-of-fact. Every place we played, you'd see the flyer with the picture of Reagan with a dick coming out of his mouth or whatever. Doing it felt like we would be preaching to the choir. I was more interested in what was happening to me personally and writing about that. I was a young man starting to grow up, experiencing things with personal relationships and friendships, and I wanted to write about it.

Above: An impassioned Dan gives the performance his all, c. 1982.

Below: Erik plays live at an early Die Kreuzen gig, c.1982.
Photos: Murray Kapell.

Erik: We just didn't feel like participating in that. For plenty of people in that scene it was the obvious thing to do, but for us it was more about the music itself. It didn't always have to have a political agenda. We definitely got some shit for it from a couple of bands, because they felt like that was the most important thing, but that wasn't why we were into the music.

Keith: We weren't interested in trying to make a political statement, which in hindsight I think helped prevent the music from dating itself. I remember reading interviews with bands where they would say things like, "Everything in life is political," and essentially saying that bands who didn't live up to their ideals weren't good enough. We never really tried, and if we had we could have very well fallen flat on our faces and ended up just another band screaming about how much they hated Ronald Reagan.

Early scene reports in fanzines helped spark interest in the band beyond their local scene, due in part to the availability of their demo cassette. Talk spread and buzz grew, resulting in more opportunities to play shows further away from Milwaukee.

Keith: We started playing Madison and Chicago a bit. I think around then we played with Hüsker Dü at the Starship.

Dan: We played with Flipper and the Zero Boys at the Starship, and Paul Mahern from the Zero Boys really liked us and asked if we would be on this compilation that he was putting out.

The Zero Boys from Indianapolis were, much like Die Kreuzen, a young hardcore punk band trying to find their footing in the Midwest. It wasn't long before similarly-minded bands began to find themselves and word spread that musically interesting things were happening in the Midwest.

Ian MacKaye: For the most part, kids who got interested in punk had nothing to work with. If you wanted to have a scene, you had to fuckin' well form one. That meant they had to form their own bands and find places to play. And those bands were drinking the water from the region, so whatever was in the region was really informing the music. If you look at a band like the Big Boys from Austin, their response to the crisis of culture was to make the music they were making. It was regionally specific because there was no cross-pollination to speak of. It was great to see the differences from town to town. In some cases, some towns kind of lagged behind. The Midwest had a lot of small and fertile micro-scenes there.

When I think about the early '80s, there was this constellation of scenes, and there were a lot of peers. You had Corey Rusk in Detroit, Al Barile in Boston, Vic Bondi in Chicago, Kevin Seconds in Reno, the Big Boys in Austin . . . they were all peers. I definitely look at Die Kreuzen as peers, people who were one of us.

Paul Mahern (singer, Zero Boys): We were the only band in our town that was venturing into playing hardcore in Indiana at the time, so all of our kindred spirits were other bands in the Midwest—Toxic Reasons in Dayton, Die Kreuzen in Milwaukee, the Effigies in Chicago—even though they were all hours away from us, I felt like all of us were part of the same scene.

The regionalism of hardcore punk created a desire for people to document what was happening in their local scenes. SST Records was documenting the scene in Southern California, and Dischord Records was doing the same in Washington, D.C. Other labels put out compilations that highlighted a slew of artists from a region on one release. With the same mindset, Mahern decided to organize a compilation LP that showcased his favorite hardcore punk bands in the Midwest called *The Master Tape*.

Paul Mahern: The *Decline of Western Civilization* LP had come out, *This Is Boston Not L.A.* had come out, and I just kinda thought that we needed to have something like that for the Midwest. The *Charred Remains* compilation had come out as a cassette, and that documented some of those bands, but I wanted to release one as an LP. I just wanted to highlight all the bands from here that I loved.

David Pajo (member, Slint, Tortoise, Gang of Four): The Midwest just had such a cool hardcore scene happening at the time. Nobody sounded like Die Kreuzen or the Crucifucks or the Zero Boys. They were all so different and so unique. It's funny, though, because I often notice that a lot of these hardcore anthologies often gloss over the Midwest, especially the Touch and Go scene, which is a bummer.

Mahern reached out to the band and set a date to have the band come down and record a few songs. Not long after, the band took a trip down to Indianapolis.

Paul Mahern: We went down to a studio owned by John Helms who recorded the Zero Boys LP. At the time, it was my goal to learn how to become a studio engineer. In putting together the *Master Tape* comp, I got all these bands to come down to Indianapolis to record there and learned

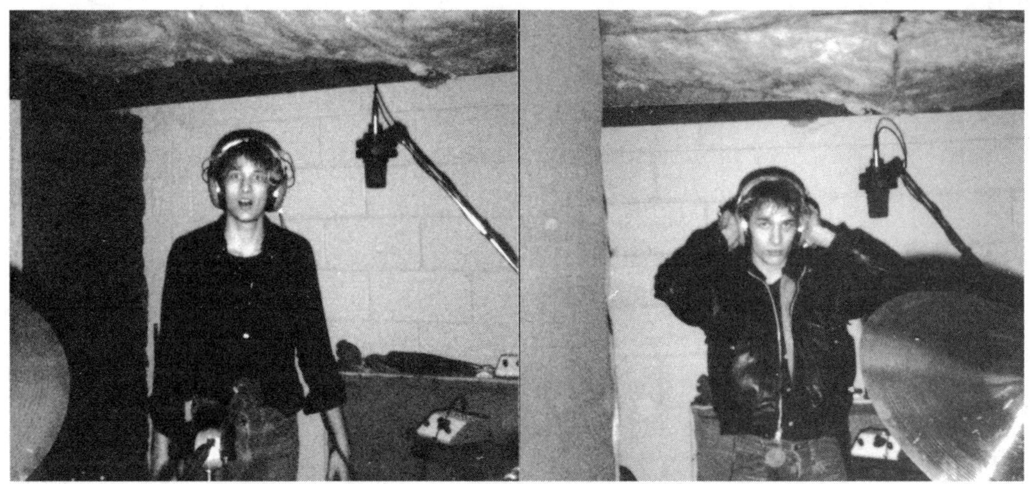

Above: Dan as he records his vocals, c. 1983.

Below: Dan showing off his onstage agility, 1983.
Photos courtesy of Die Kreuzen. Photographers unknown.

as his intern in the process of making the *Master Tape*. It doubled as my education on how to become a record producer.

Dan: We played in Chicago and drove down to Indianapolis afterwards.

Keith: It was the dead of winter, and we were riding in a car with no heat, and it was just totally fucking Arctic. But we eventually got there and knocked the songs out in an afternoon pretty much. Just bashed 'em out, it was really quick.

Mahern's decision to create a document of Midwestern hardcore punk gave opportunity to many bands who at the time had little beyond homemade demo cassettes for sale. Its songs range from midtempo rockers to faster tracks that are more in line with the post-Circle Jerks set. Two of Die Kreuzen's three selections, "Fighting" and "On the Street," find them continuing to push the boundaries of speed and intensity, while the third, "All White," shows their ability to go from a sludgy dirge to a proto-power violence level of chaos.

Between their demo and appearances on both the *Charred Remains* and *Master Tape* compilations, Die Kreuzen was making a name for themselves beyond the Midwest. The goal was to reach as many people as possible, so the band began to slowly venture farther away from the Great Lakes, playing in as many cities as their car would take them to.

Brad Wood: First time I saw them in Milwaukee, it was just super-tight and fast and short. Keith was definitely the focal point because he's just the coolest fucking person to ever hold a bass—he was just born to pick up a Rickenbacker.

Keith: We'd play in all these unlikely places; we just really wanted to play. It was around then that we started to get familiar with the experience of just playing anywhere that would have us. Our friend Scott Colburn would set us up in Bloomington, Indiana. It was an "okay come down, you can play in this church hall, my dad is a reverend" kind of thing, and then they'd let us stay in their house afterwards, feed us, and all that. We were appreciative of it, because back then you just stayed wherever, so when it was a nicer arrangement we really appreciated it.

Brian: The scene in Milwaukee was definitely good, but no one was really promoting it [outside of Milwaukee] because no one really knew there was a scene here.

A flyer for a 1984 show at Niko's (Milwaukee), featuring Die Kreuzen and Chicago's Articles of Faith.

Steve Albini [Recording Engineer and guitarist/singer, Big Black, Shellac]: The Midwest punk scenes in their beginnings were extremely eclectic, much more than the West Coast punk scenes who formalized very quickly. In Chicago at that time, there were performance-art collectives. In Chicago there was a really big queer crossover where the venues and promoters and people involved in the punk scene were also involved in the gay underground and the gay bar scene. There wasn't a kind of homogenization in the Midwestern scenes. There was a collecting impulse where all the freaks from all corners of the city would find themselves at a punk show and realize that they could be as odd or outlandish as they wanted there, and it would be okay.

Keith: Pretty much every single band in Milwaukee was doing something different at the time. No one really sounded the same. You had the Ama-Dots, the Oil Tasters, the Prosecutors, the Sidewalks, and the Shivvers. There were just all these bands doing different things and I think a lot of people didn't know exactly what to make of it all. Audiences were really fixated on out-of-town bands, especially bands from New York, but they didn't take the whole West Coast hardcore thing too seriously.

Steve Albini: Specifically, when I think of the Milwaukee bands from that time period, like the Haskels and the Oil Tasters and Couch Flambeau, none of them were stereotypical. There were other bands like Hollywood Autopsy and the Ama-Dots, and all of these bands had this artier aspect to them. There was a conceptual aspect to all these bands that was beyond just fitting into a sound or whatever. If you were a young band getting involved in the music scene, your role models or peers would all be open-minded people who all had a lot of different creative vectors going on. And that wasn't the case in a lot of the more cosmopolitan places.

Brian: We'd keep in touch with other bands we'd play with and just kinda ask them how they were able to do it and then they'd give us contact information for clubs or bands that could help us out. We'd play with Articles of Faith in Chicago. We'd play Madison with Mecht Mensch and the Tar Babies. We knew we weren't going to get anywhere sitting around in Milwaukee.

Erik: We started playing out of town a lot. The Effigies invited us to Chicago to play with them, or we'd go up to Minneapolis and play with Hüsker Dü.

Dan: We were traveling in a four-door Impala. It was huge. We somehow managed to fit most of Erik's drums in the back. The person sitting in the back would have to put their feet on top of an amplifier, and the person riding up front would have a floor tom on their lap, but we somehow made it work with all four of us in there with the guitars in the back window.

Keith: We eventually graduated to vans. We were lucky that Erik was able to work on them. We would have been screwed without him.

To say that Tunison's mechanic skills helped the band would be an understatement. Touring musicians put an incredible amount of wear and tear on their vehicles, especially punk bands in the eighties who relied on a fleet of well-loved vans from the late sixties and early seventies. Tunison's ability to work on cars proved to be a blessing on more than a few occasions.

Dan: I watched him take apart the starter of our van, examine each tiny piece until he figured out which part was broke, get the replacement part, put it back together, and put it back in the van.

Keith: I watched him crawl under the van and fix broken parts in the pouring rain at night.

Erik: A person can get highly motivated when you're pushing a truck through the desert. There were plenty of times when I was able to fix the problem, but there were times when I just wasn't able to get it together. I had tools, and I was the one that was the most mechanically oriented out of the band. But yeah, there were definitely times when it ended up working out and I looked like the hero.

In their first year of activity, Die Kreuzen had already accomplished a number of their goals, from playing on impressive bills to releasing a killer demo and appearing on a handful of compilations. It was a strong beginning for them, but playing the same clubs to the same people over and over again wasn't cutting it. They wanted more than what Milwaukee could offer, as the scene wasn't as organized or developed enough to support an independent record label. Homemade demo cassettes and inclusions on compilations proved to be limited in reaching new listeners. The band needed to record a release of their own. ●

Above: One of the band's many tour vans.

Below: Die Kreuzen's resident mechanic Erik fixes the van, one of many times. Photos courtesy of Die Kreuzen.

Caption: Erik, somewhere in Europe, c. 1987. Courtesy of Die Kreuzen. Photographer unknown.

Cows and Beer

ARTISTS INTERESTED IN RELEASING ANYTHING BEYOND home-made demo cassettes were often left with no affordable options, but the fortunate ones caught the attention of small independent labels, looking to release seven-inch EPs. Die Kreuzen's well-received demo cassettes and growing reputation as a fierce live act began to produce results. People were now asking to release their music.

Keith: The *Master Tape* comp came out, and that turned out well, and we were on a couple of cassette compilations too. This guy Bob Moore [owner, Version Sound Records] heard the cassettes. He contacted us and said that he wanted to release a seven-inch of ours. We had no money and no way of putting out our own record, but we knew a girl who was training to become a recording engineer and needed something to record. She offered to record us for free as a part of her final project. She was working at this studio called Traum Studios. We got in touch with Bob, and he laid it all out for us where he'd pay for the pressing and give us half of the records. We just went in and did it really quick, blasting it out live in a few hours. We sent off the tapes and art, and a few months later we got a box of records.

Richard Kohl: I was a fine-arts major in college, but I dropped out and kept doing a lot of drawing. Living at the Norman I just spent a lot of time working on my art. They saw some of that and were just like, "Well, why don't you draw something for us?"

A lot of hardcore bands at the time had no money and thus the album art often looked shitty, or it all looked the same. I didn't want my work to be part of any of that—that seemed to represent something a little substandard to me. Still, there was creativity in some hardcore records, like how Black Flag had all that great Raymond Pettibon art. If it was going to have my name on it, I wanted it to look good because I knew that people were going to see it.

If memory serves, I believe the title came first. I don't remember them giving me too many directives—I just came up with it. Back in those days I did everything with pen and ink. You could get these really nice technical pens called Radiographs that were made in Germany, and they were engineered really well. They came with all these different-sized points, and I'd use the really small one and just do a lot of cross action. I just put the cow on the back there to reflect the title they gave me.

Having the financial backing of a label made it possible for the EP to happen, but for all intents and purposes this was still a DIY affair. If the band wanted covers to go with the records, they had to print and assemble them on their own.

Keith: We had the records, but we didn't have any plastic inner sleeves. We couldn't afford to buy new ones, so we just pillaged our record collection for sleeves and sat at Erik's mom's house folding the inserts.

Erik: They [the records] showed up in the paper sleeves and we printed the covers locally. A lot of them still had price tags and stamps on there that said "Peaches" and "Record Head" or whatever places we were getting records from at the time.

Keith: Actually, having a physical record was so significant back then.

Dan: It was like, "Wow, holy shit, I've got my own record."

Erik: I'm still knocked out by the reception that we get for *Cows and Beer*. We put a lot of work into that record, and we were really happy with how that struck people.

***Cows and Beer* marked another evolutionary step in their sound, as the improved fidelity was a considerable upgrade from what they could produce themselves. From a modern-day perspective, *Cows and Beer* may sound like the work of a student recording engineer, but all too often the most important element of any great recording is capturing performances from great players.**

Be it the Bad Brains *ROIR* cassette, Black Flag's *Nervous Breakdown*, or Minor Threat's debut EP, all of these recordings are brilliant in their own right. Though none of the releases could be considered hi-fi recordings, the strength of the performances brightly outshines their simplified production.

Such is the case with *Cows and Beer*, its six tracks clocking in just shy of seven minutes. There was no opportunity to spend days on a vocal take; what is captured here is raw and vicious but, much like the demo recordings, incredibly precise. Kubinski's tongue-in-cheek-intro of "Yo mama" kicks off the EP, which pummels the listener from track to track. The arrangements and performances of the tracks differ only slightly from their previous demo versions, yet it's still clear that various things had been trimmed, tweaked, and adjusted for efficiency and impact. Each track is noticeably faster this time around, but it doesn't sound like any member is struggling to keep up. Every element feels intentional, and nothing feels out of place.

Die Kreuzen had built enough of a fanbase and buzz that the 7" was popular among punk cognoscenti. Reviews show a largely positive critical response from fanzines at the time. In his "Puszone" column for *Thrasher*, Pushead called it a "superb EP of tremendous ability." *Wireless* fanzine called them "the only thrash band that matters," noting the EP's distinctive qualities that separated them from many of their peers. *Maximum Rocknroll* also noted its complexity, saying, "Die Kreuzen provide further proof that the Midwest is no longer slumbering."

Thurston Moore: I had the *Cows and Beer* record because I bought any hardcore seven-inch that was being released at the time. Living in New York then, it was easy to get most any record you wanted because you had record stores that prided themselves on carrying any independent record from anywhere. There was this store called Rat Cage, which was kind of the meeting point for people who were into hardcore, and they definitely had it.

I was really interested in what was happening in the Midwest with bands like the Necros and Negative Approach, to me those records were the best. They had this energy that I just felt like was the real voice of what was going on in middle America at the time. It didn't have all this kind of glamor that New York or Los Angeles or San Francisco had historically. There was something much cooler about that. Suddenly it was just like taking away the celebrity of being in the city. Hardcore was really specializing in that. It was taking initiative, in that you didn't have to go to New York to become something. You didn't have to go anywhere to become something; you could stay local. It was an important political thing. I was really interested in that concept.

Damian Abraham (singer, Fucked Up; host, *Turned Out a Punk* podcast): Hardcore and punk at times can leave behind the fact that it's outsider music, and then it becomes a little bit like sports or something. *Cows and Beer* felt like outsider music. When you hear that record, it doesn't seem like there's a Dischord or some sort of clubhouse they're going back to and palling around with; it feels like it was made by people who were on their own.

The Stooges are the ultimate outsider band, and bands who have that Stooges gateway, you can really hear that in their music. They're on this island unto themselves, just like the kid in the back of class who doesn't fit in. You read lyrics like "Hate Me" or "In School," it feels like that same kid sitting in the back of the class, carving band logos into their desk and always getting into trouble.

Not long after its release, the band appeared on a public-access television special called *Who Am I: The Punk Rock Attitude*. It was a half-hour presentation about the growing punk and hardcore scene in Milwaukee which featured an interview with the band as well as Nik Stathus, the proprietor of a short-lived venue in Milwaukee called Niko's. Dressed in a professional manner, the host, Liz Weiss, seemed to have a genuine curiosity about the band and the genre at large. Based on her questions, Weiss and a majority of the viewing audience were likely unfamiliar with hardcore punk, but she still asked thoughtful questions about topics like violence at shows, the local Milwaukee music scene, their inspirations and familial backgrounds. At times, the band members speak over each other, but the interview shows the members exactly as they were at the time, just a bunch of guys from the Midwest. Being interviewed for anything beyond a punk fanzine at this time was a rarity, and the band handles the interview segment quite well.

The band's performance here is a priceless artifact of the time. It's especially significant as there isn't a sizable amount of video footage from this period, much less footage that was intended for public consumption. The band ripped through an impressive eleven-song set, taking little to no breaks in between. Even this early on in their career, it's apparent how well-rehearsed and tight the band was. The performance is blistering: Brammer and Tunison rip through rhythms with stylish confidence, Egeness's guitar squeals and

Above: The iconic Die Kreuzen cow logo, used early on in the band's career on hats and stickers. Courtesy of Die Kreuzen.

Below: The interview portion of Die Kreuzen's legendary public-access television performance, 1983. Photo: Kevin Hutchison.

moans as he manipulates it to his will, while the beginnings of Kubinski's signature throat-shattering scream are on full display. The fact that something as abrasive and challenging as this performance aired on local Milwaukee television in 1983 is still difficult to comprehend. Over time, this footage became a rarity among tape traders and collectors alike, eventually finding its way to YouTube, where it has received over 100,000 combined views as of 2025. This performance is truly revered by Die Kreuzen fans, with some holding it in as high esteem as any of the band's studio recordings.

Keith: They [the show producer] just called us up and asked if we wanted to be on this public-access thing, and we were like, "Yeah, sure." We just went down there and winged it—it's not like we practiced specifically for it. It was really simple—we just set up our equipment the way we always did and hoped that it wouldn't fall over, because they had us set up on this really unstable platform. We practiced the same way, only we jumped around a lot more when we actually played. There was no premeditation; it was just our set at the time.

Erik: We played probably everything [every song] we had at the time.

MaryJo Tunison (wife of Erik Tunison): I had to go over to my grandmother's house to watch that. We were so poor and our TV broke, and my mom was saving up to buy another one. So I walked over to my grandmother's house to watch him. I was so proud of them, so proud.

Richard Kohl: I was telling all my family to tune in. I remember telling my dad, "You gotta tune in tonight to see this band that I'm working with," and I was so proud to see them on TV playing and everything. Afterwards I called my dad, and I was so excited, and I was like, "What didja think?" and totally deadpan he just says to me, "What *zoo* did you find these people in?" But I quickly realized that if my dad hated it, then it must be good.

For all the work that they out into refining their sound, the band felt the limitations of Milwaukee's small scene, as there were only so many clubs, VFW halls, and church basememnts in the area that they could play.

Keith: There used to be these bowling alleys or whatever on the south side at the time, basically just old houses. Most of them would have a big room upstairs, so we'd have Erik go in and say, "Hey, we wanna have a private party here," and then we'd book whoever. Generally, those were only good for one show a piece, because once the show would happen they'd be freaked out by a million kids at the show, hanging around drinking outside or whatever. We had shows at a lot of places like that or VFW halls.

Richard Kohl: There were other bands and younger bands who were playing in Church halls and bowling alleys—places that were cheap and easy to rent but also dumpy. A lot of churches on the south side of Milwaukee almost always had a church hall to rent, and it would be, like, maybe $15 to rent it for an event. I'd go into these churches with Erik and we'd be like, "We play in this band, we play really loud music, this is what is going to be happening, there's gonna be a few people but not a whole lot," and the priests would just be like, "Well, can you pay us the $15 now?"

Most of those shows were all-ages; Milwaukee had a tight curfew. The second time MDC played through town and I rented out another one of these church halls, I told them that we had to be done by a certain time or the cops were gonna show up. Of course, the show ran late, and the cops did show up.

Dan: We would play Niko's a lot, and it was there that we met MDC when they came to Milwaukee for the first time. They stayed with us at the Norman, and the next morning I got up and started talking to Dave [Dictor] about touring, wondering how they were able to get shows out of town.

He just opened up this book he had and started talking: "There's this guy in Austin called Mikey Donaldson who plays bass in a band called the Offenders—if you get a hold of him, he can get you a show there and maybe Houston and San Antonio too. And then here is a guy from JFA—he'll get you a show in Phoenix. It's hard to get a show in L.A., but if you get a hold of this guy Tom from Golden Voice, he might be able to help you out." And he just spelled it out for me like that, with people to play with and stay with. That's where our first batch of contacts came from, basically. He just opened up his information phone book for me and said, "Here you go," and that was it.

Ian MacKaye: For touring bands, there were these phone lists that you'd have photocopies of. One of the lists had a bunch of people in different towns who could either get you a gig or put you in touch with someone else who could. I bet you Dan was probably on some of those lists. The other lists had corporate phone numbers, places like Coca-Cola, Exxon, the American Nazi Party, places like that. At that time, answering machines were not really common, especially for companies. Back then, you'd book your tour by calling from a payphone after ten p.m. You'd charge the call to your home phone, but instead of giving them your actual home phone number you'd give them one of these numbers you had on the list. If they told you that it wasn't a home number and actually a company number, then you'd draw a line through it on the list, photocopy that, and hand out the updated one. The number-one rule was to only call from a payphone and never a home phone, because that way it couldn't be traced.

In a pre-internet, pre-streaming era, geography was much more significant for how bands found their audiences. Die Kreuzen wanted to entirely relocate to a city with a larger and more supportive music scene, specifically one that could support a hardcore punk band. In the early '80s, the biggest hardcore punk scenes were on the east and west coasts, with both New York and L.A. boasting vibrant communities of bands and concert goers alike. New York's hardcore scene was a reflection of the city at the time, as was the music, with acts like Agnostic Front, the Cro-Mags and Cause for Alarm all taking cues from Bad Brains (who themselves relocated from Washington, D.C., to New York in 1981) and combining them with a darker and meaner edge. Los Angeles was home to the Germs, Black Flag, X, Circle Jerks, and so many other key figures in early-'80s American punk and hardcore. While New York's hardcore punk scene had a more unified look and sound, the L.A. scene in the early '80s was a bit more diverse, and the aesthetics in both style and sonics were harder to pin down. With this in mind, it's not surprising that Die Kreuzen had their hearts set on relocating to L.A., a city with an eclectic but thriving scene of acts that their music could easily fit into.

Keith: We hadn't played the East Coast at all, so we weren't familiar with any of the things that were happening out there. We mainly played the Midwest and the extended Midwest. We played with tons of bands—most of them no one had ever heard of because we'd go out and it would end up being in someone's living room or whatever. There were very few clubs that anybody played at. Eventually we got people talking a bit, so we decided to move out to L.A. because we thought we could actually make a living out there and be successful.

We had heard about all these bands playing to, like, a thousand people, and we were stuck here playing to, like, forty people or whatever. The Starship closed, and for a while there weren't too many places to play. And then Niko's started and that only existed for less than a year and we were back to having no place to play.

Richard Kohl: Not long after the Starship closed, my friend Darren Andres had the brilliant smarts and luck to find this place Niko's. He walks into this empty place and starts talking to the bartender who's also the owner. It was a nice-sized place, it had a good stage that was probably three or four feet off the stage, so you could see the band from wherever you were in the bar, and this guy is crying in his beer because nobody was coming to his bar anymore. He called me immediately and I went down there right away. I told him that I'd guarantee him a bar, and then we'd take the door—real easy, nothing complicated. We did pretty good there. The other good thing was that he didn't know any of the bands anyway, so we took to booking anyone we wanted. We ruled that place a little bit, and it was a good venue to have when touring bands were coming through town. Meat Puppets played there, MDC played there—not a whole lot but some. That lasted for about a year. After a while the owner got to be a bit much to deal with.

Keith: Really, we just got fed up and decided to leave. In our minds it was like, "All right, we're just gonna live in L.A.—it's gotta be cool there."

Brian: The scene here was definitely good, but no one was really promoting because no one really knew there was a scene here. We'd keep in touch with other bands we'd play with and just kinda ask them how they were able to do it, and then they'd give us contact information for clubs or bands that could help us out. We just started calling people; we had every intention of moving out to L.A.

Dan: I wrote down a bunch of the contacts that I got from Dave and then gave that info to Richard Kohl and just let him go with it. One day I came home from work and he said, "Well, I talked to that Mikey guy in Austin and got you some shows in Austin and San Antonio," and it made me feel like it was for real now, like something was actually starting to happen for us.

Over time and with the help of the growing network of bands and venues throughout the country, Die Kreuzen put together their first major tour. Using the contacts they got from Dave, the self-proclaimed "Tour for Life" was booked.

Keith: We went down to Texas, and I believe we ended up staying in Austin for at least a few days with the Offenders.

Dan: They got us a show in New Orleans and that was the first time we played with them.

Above: A marquee for a New Orleans gig featuring Die Kreuzen and Austin, Texas, hardcore heroes the Offenders.

Below: The band plays a living room in Kansas City during the "Tour for Life," June 1983. Photos: Richard Kohl.

Keith: We had a couple of friends that used to live here that had moved out to L.A. They lived right off Hollywood Boulevard. We went down there when we got in to try and get something to eat, and almost immediately some dude was trying to sell us dope. We were so surprised by how seedy and gross it was.

We were playing at the Cathay Degrande, and we pulled up to the venue to load our equipment. Literally about forty seconds later this cop comes up and gives us a $50 ticket. We were all confused and he was like, "You can't park here," and we were just like, "We're from Wisconsin, it doesn't say that you can't park here," and he was just like, "Yeah, well, everyone knows you can't park here," and just left.

Eventually we went in, play the show, and it was actually a good show. We went and stayed with our friends at this apartment, and by that point we decided that we didn't want to live there. There weren't any inexpensive places to rehearse. We had a couple of other shows booked, and the people we were staying with were making crystal meth out of starter fluid and shit.

Dan: The whole apartment complex smelled like it was going to explode. Like if someone lit a match that would've been it.

Keith: The next day we played with the Flower Leopards, which was Tony from the Adolescents' new band at the time.

Dan: After that show, we decided that we'd just go to San Francisco, because that was where Richard wanted to go anyway, as our friend Angie had moved out there.

Keith: We played a show at the Mabuhay Gardens, which went well. We ran into this guy who was in Code of Honor who had a show at the end of the month. They wanted us to play that show, which supposedly was going to pay well and all that. The problem was that by that point we had run completely out of money, so we were pretty much down for whatever. We had to decide what we were going to do for a month because we had no place to stay. Thankfully, we met Mike [Arredondo] and QE [Kieth].

Brian: Mike and QE introduced themselves to us at a show. They were kind enough to put us up until we could try and find jobs.

Erik: We absolutely would have been homeless if not for them. They allowed us the opportunity to stay there for a bit and play some shows.

Keith: They let us stay with them at their house for the entire month basically, and we did what we always did, which was clean up the place and do dishes and whatnot.

The help of friends saved the four band members as they tried to figure out what they were going to do. Photos of Die Kreuzen in San Francisco taken by Arredondo appear in a rare 1984 book titled *Loud 3D*. Arredondo and the photographers Gary Robert and Rob Kulakofsky assembled a collection of three-dimensional live photos of punk and hardcore bands in the early '80s. Aside from Die Kreuzen, Minor Threat, Black Flag, 7 Seconds, and Dead Kennedys all appear in this now highly collectible book. Photos from this era exist largely within the confines of record sleeves and fanzines, but this collection of largely "action shot" style photos that come to life with the use of 3D glasses is well worth the asking price. Among the rarer artifacts from this time period, *Loud 3D* is perhaps the most singular of them, existing somewhere in between a DIY photo fanzine and an abstract art piece.

Keith: By that point we had come to the conclusion that we weren't going to be able to stay there [San Francisco] because it was just too expensive. We really didn't have any money; we were just counting on this show at the end of the month to get us enough money to get home.

Dan: We did a couple of gigs during that month, maybe one or two, just so we could get by until the end of the month.

Keith: I remember the Tool and Die [Valencia Tool & Die, a San Francisco nightclub]—people always talk about that place. It was like a storefront—there was a hole in the front, and there was a ladder that you had to haul your stuff down. It was like a concrete basement. If there was any kind of fire situation, everyone would've been dead.

Dan: We played at the Mabuhay Gardens at least twice, so we had just barely enough money to live until the end of the month.

Keith: Jello Biafra was at one of the Mab shows. I remember talking with him about Lalo Schifrin soundtracks for a long time.

The band entertained any offers they could to play a show, no matter how unorthodox the gig was.

Dan: One of my favorite bands on the *Not so Quiet on the Western Front* compilation was this band called the Naked Lady Wrestlers. Die Kreuzen played in S.F. at the Tool and Die, and I think they played with us—I know Los Olvidados did for sure. At the very least, one of the members of Naked Lady Wrestlers was there, and I was introduced to him. He's kind of a smartass dude and said to me, "Oh, you guys got nothing going on Saturday night? We've got a show up in Petaluma playing this college party. You guys should come up—there's gonna be beer and food—probably get you some money." We didn't have anything going on at the time, so he gave us the address.

Saturday came around and we decided that we were gonna play the show, so we hopped in the truck with our gear and drove up to Petaluma. I remember the directions took us up onto this bluff that overlooks the ocean. I remember on the west side of the bluff there was this convenience-store gas-station kinda thing, and on the other side of the road there was this nondescript building that was a rental hall. We pull up, it matches the address, so we decided to go inside.

We get inside, and there's like four big dudes wearing sheets like togas. They got a keg of beer and they wanted to charge us each a dollar a cup to go in, and we were like, "Actually, we're the band," and they were like, "Really? Okay! Come set up," and they take us to where the stage is. We set up, have a few beers, and no one's coming. Naked Lady Wrestlers didn't show.

I have no idea what happened with that, but eventually someone was like, "Hey, are you guys gonna play or what?" and there's, like, you know, maybe five dudes there, all wearing togas. We were like, "Sure," and we just released on 'em. I remember one guy was standing there with beer, watching us with his eyes wide open. They were receptive to it; I don't think they'd probably heard anything like it or knew what it was. I think it was probably just shocking to them.

Keith: I think about it now, because we had no place to practice but these shows to play. We literally had nothing but downtime for the most part. It was definitely better than L.A., but it was still incredibly expensive. It was like, "Where's a good place to practice?" and they'd be like, "Oh, you can practice in these abandoned beer vats for $40 an hour."

Dan: At that time, [the waiting] felt like an eternity, especially spending that much time in someone else's home. We were all just in this room with a TV. We watched a lot of MTV because it was still new at the time.

We were seeing old Cheap Trick videos and stuff.

Keith: We spent a lot of it just wandering around San Francisco. I remember one time we took acid and went down to Fisherman's Wharf.

Brian: We took Black Pyramid acid, which was supposed to be split into fourths, but we didn't know that.

Erik: Keith and I chose to listen to the advice of the person who gave it to us: "Maybe try half first and then the other half later." Half was more than enough. I don't think the other guys took their advice.

Keith: We were just standing there, staring at the Bay Bridge, laughing so hard [laughs].

Brian: There was a huge water maze down there, so we started walking around through it. I got lost—it seemed like an eternity before I found them. We decided from there to walk to Fisherman's Wharf.

Erik: We were walking down Market Street through the Tenderloin and that's when we were really starting to trip. It was pretty rough down there—strip clubs, porn theaters, trash in the streets.

Keith: We were walking home down Market Street at, like, two in the morning and we're like, "Hey look at that guy, he looks like a cop," and we all start laughing, and then we get closer and realized, "Oh shit, that's a cop!"

Dan: He was this huge beat cop who looked like he'd been on the streets forever—big scar on his face—real tough looking guy.

Keith: We were all like, "Quick, act straight!" and of course that wasn't happening. We might as well have had signs over our heads that said "I'm fucked up" on it.

Dan: He was walking up to us twirling his nightstick, picking up trash, and batting it into the street. And there we were, tripping our brains out.

Keith: The cop comes up to us, twirling his baton, and he's like, "Where you boys headed to?" and I'm not even sure how, but before we could even say anything . . .

Dan: Erik just looked at the cop and in the politest voice said to him, "175 Duncan, sir."

Erik: 175 Duncan! The cop gave us the directions, sent us on our way.

Dan: No trouble at all—the cop just looked at us and said, "All right, you boys, have a good night."

Luckily, we had a little bit of money in the band kitty. Keith was our chef for the month. That's how Keith kept busy. He was always making dough to make bread or figuring out whatever way to make potatoes. Keith was always cooking.

Keith: We basically lived on potatoes for an entire month. We'd go buy big bags of potatoes, slice them up, fry them, or bake them. We'd pretty much eat potatoes and drink Brown Derby beer.

Brian: [laughs] Just a *lot* of potatoes and a lot of beer. Brown Derby Beer seemed to be the favorite amongst the band back then.

Keith: Every once in a while for a treat we'd go to this place called El Toro. It was the first place we had ever been that had giant burritos; they were so humongous that they could last you for like two days. That place was absolutely delicious.

Dan: Erik and I took a lot of walks, because it was free and [we were] in this cool hilly area. One time we decided to take a walk, but it was super-foggy, and we couldn't see the top of the peak that we usually walked to. We decided to go anyway, and at one point we got above the clouds while standing on this little grassy knoll. I remember the fog clearing on this little piece of knoll, but we couldn't see any of the city below us.

Brian was always practicing, just playing guitar with no amp all the time. He was always playing and practicing. He knew all those Van Halen and Metal Church records by heart. Just for hours, playing guitar.

Kinda sitting around on their floor, I think we realized that we couldn't stay in California. I remember when we played with X at the Starship, I was talking to John Doe and Exene, and I was talking about how we wanted to move out to L.A., and to my surprise, they didn't think it was a good idea. They pulled me aside and they were like, "You don't wanna move to L.A., dude. You guys are a good band., You should stay here and be a big fish in a little pond. You guys go out to L.A., and you'll be a small fish in a big pond, and they'll just eat you up." That conversation came to the forefront of my mind when we finally decided to get out of San Francisco.

Keith: We were just waiting for that show at the end of the month, and then, not too long before it was supposed to happen, we found out from one of the Code of Honor guys that we couldn't play the show anymore for whatever reason.

Brian: We were going to play with Code of Honor, and their guitarist came over that afternoon and solidified it. He just told us to show up and we'd be able to play. We had parked on the side of the Mab in the alley and started unloading, and we got our gear about three steps to the door when the club owner came up to us like, "Who the fuck are you?" Turns out no one talked to the promoter about it, and he wasn't too happy about that and told us that we couldn't play. We were trying to figure out how we were going to get back home, because that show was going to provide us with the gas money to get back home to Wisconsin.

Erik: We had been in touch with Tim Yohannan, because he had interviewed us. I called him up letting him know that we had been looking for shows, and he just gave me Jello Biafra's phone number. I called him and he picked up the phone! He told me to call him back in a few days.

Brian: Tim and Jello came out of the On Broadway. We told them our situation and Jello just told us to wait. He left for maybe five or ten minutes, came back, and said, "Okay, you're going to play right before us at the On Broadway, and we'll give you $500 to get you back home to Milwaukee."

Keith: It was this gigantic theater above the Mabuhay that held like a thousand-plus people. We probably made like five times as much on that show than what we probably would have made had we played that first show, so that was nice.

Dan: It was great. I think the show was with Dead Kennedys, D.O.A., Crucifix, the Feeders, and Personality Crisis.

Erik: Jello was really kind and helpful. In fact, every show we played with the Kennedys over the years was always pretty good. They would settle up with the promoter and then pay the openers themselves, and they paid the support acts pretty well. We got paid better by them than we did directly from club owners for a long time. They were a really good bunch of guys.

Brian: It was amazing. He was like Jesus for us that day. Thank you, Jello.

The kindness of Jello Biafra provided them with what was needed to go back home. Kohl stayed in San Francisco, as was his plan the entire time,

though he continued to work with the group in one form or another.

During the interim, Tunison booked a handful of shows for the band on the way back to Milwaukee, with stops in Salt Lake City, Denver, Kansas City, and others.

Keith: We played a show in Reno in a storage locker.

Dan: We stayed at Kevin Seconds' house for a weekend. I remember sitting on his couch and reading this Star Wars book, like, the whole time. His mom was awesome, too. She cooked for us.

Erik: Mom Seconds made us chili mac? Lasagna? Something like that—she definitely took care of us.

Keith: It was the best dinner we had had in months!

We weren't fighting any more than usual. You put four twenty-one-year-old guys and haul them across the country, yeah, there's gonna be disagreements.

The band's plan to relocate to the West Coast ended with them having no choice but to return home. They managed to play to a handful of new audiences and alongside Dead Kennedys, one of the biggest bands in the underground at the time. For a first tour, things could have gone a lot worse. Still, the band's initial plan of moving to California had fallen through, and they were unable to make it work. Tired and broke, they finally found their way back home to Milwaukee.

Then they broke up. ●

Keith and Erik, c. 1982. Courtesy of Die Kreuzen, photographer unknown.

The Debut Album

AFTER RETURNING HOME FROM CALIFORNIA, THE BAND HAD fragmented. The life of a touring musician is never easy, and the extended time away from home had taken its toll. The experiences didn't measure up to what they had hoped for, and after finding their way back to the Midwest the future of the band was uncertain.

Keith: We came back to Milwaukee, but it wasn't like we were defeated or anything like that. It just wasn't realistic for us to be able to survive out there, so we came back. And Brian promptly quit upon us coming home.

Brian: The California experience made me not really want to be in the band. It was a grueling experience. It was exciting but depressing—it was a lot to take on. We weren't getting along on the way back home, and a lot of it probably had to do with us not being able to eat. We didn't succeed how we were hoping to succeed, and I was pretty depressed about it. I just seriously needed to get away and think about what I wanted to do. I worked and skateboarded and just hung out really.

Keith: We decided to try out some other guitar players, but none of them really worked out too well for us. After that, I decided I wasn't going to play in the band anymore either.

Dan sits outside of the Norman in Milwaukee as pedestrians pass by, c. 1983. Photo: Kevin Hutchison.

Dan: I went back to living at the Norman. I played with Erik and this guy Brian Vanderplas for a while, just working. Nothing exciting during that time.

Kubinski, Tunison, and Egeness all stayed back in Milwaukee, but Brammer used the band's split as an opportunity to leave Milwaukee and play bass for a post-punk band called the Tense Experts.

Keith: I moved to Rockford and played with the Tense Experts for a bit—a month or month and a half maybe? I got a job, and I slept in their spare room and wrote a bunch of songs with the singer of the band, Bobby Steele. Eventually it just got boring because there was nothing going on. Unbeknownst to me, Mike and Tommy Ciaccio, who played guitar and bass in the band, had girlfriends in Milwaukee. They promptly moved up there, kinda leaving me and the singer high and dry in Rockford. I was working at Taco Bell. I would walk to and from work every day, which was probably, like, a mile, just listening to REM's *Murmur* over and over on my cassette Walkman. I think I eventually just called my mom and asked her to come and get me, which was good timing because Bobby told me I couldn't stay there much longer.

Die Kreuzen could have easily been one of many early '80s hardcore acts whose sole output was a single seven-inch EP. It wasn't long before the four began talking again and eventually made the decision to reform after the short time spent apart.

Keith: After a night of living in Brookfield, I realized that I didn't want to be there. The Appliances-SFB were doing an in-store at Ludwig Van Ear Records, so I went down there and ran into Dan, who offered for me to move in with him at the Norman. I think it took about a month before we started talking about possibly playing again.

Brian: I remember calling Dan and us talking a bit about reforming.

Keith: Part of it was, before we split up, Corey Rusk from Touch and Go Records had gotten a hold of us and asked us if we wanted to do an album.

Dan: We were also asked by the guys from Golden Voice to be on *Rat Music for Rat People, Volume 2.* We had these two good things going for us, and Keith and I were definitely down for doing it again.

Keith: We contacted the rest of the guys, and no one was doing anything, and then we called Corey to see if that was still a viable offer.

Erik: We had played with the Necros before we left for tour at the Lost Dutchman's Mine. That's the first time I remember meeting Corey.

Dan: He was hanging out at my house going through my records, and the first record he saw was by a band called Savage Republic, and he was so surprised that someone in a hardcore band was into a band like that.

Enter Corey Rusk, who along with Richard Kohl came to play a continuous and integral role in the band's history. Rusk had founded Touch and Go Records with the Meatmen's Tesco Vee in 1981, originally as a fanzine before deciding to start putting out records as well.

Corey Rusk (bassist, Necros; co-founder, Touch and Go Records): In 1981, no one was going to put out your record unless it was you. I was playing in a band called the Necros at the time, and we wanted to put out a record. Tesco and Dave [Stimson] came up with the money and put out the first few releases, and from that we decided that we wanted to put out more records. I got a job and, with the little money I made from it, we went into the studio and recorded what became the nine-song Necros EP.

There was no one at the time that was interested in releasing this kind of music. Obviously, the major labels existed, but they certainly were not interested in the sort of stuff that we were interested in.

I don't know what it was about the process that I liked, but we had enthusiasm for our band and other bands in the Detroit area like Negative Approach and the Meatmen. It was an exciting time. There was a lot of interesting music being made, so starting a label just seemed like a good idea. All the records that Touch and Go put out, we were just hoping to break even. More than anything, we just wanted these records to exist. We had a passion for the music, and we wanted it to be made available for the people who wanted to hear it.

I'm sure that my first introduction to Die Kreuzen was the *Cows and Beer* EP. I thought it was really good and that they were interesting. I can't remember if it was that record specifically that made me want to work with them. What I do remember, though, is that Necros played Milwaukee with Die Kreuzen and that their live show was a mind-blowing experience for me. That was the first time I saw them and I'm sure that that was what made me think, "Oh my god, I want to work with these guys."

Their live show was just intense. There were a lot of bands that played fast and loud back then, but Die Kreuzen really had their shit together and were just super-tight, not at all sloppy. The tones of their instruments, the way they worked together—they all came together in a way that you didn't see in a lot of other bands, especially other bands who were playing that fast at the time. I was blown away by what a great live band they were. I couldn't stop thinking about their gig. They were unlike any other band at that time. They were lumped in with "hardcore" bands at the time by the press, but there was so much more going on with Die Kreuzen than just "hardcore."

When I got back home to Ohio, I called them to see if they wanted to do an album with Touch and Go. They agreed, and then promptly broke up! I was heartbroken. Needless to say, I was pleased when they reformed and got back in touch with me.

Dan: I think I got on the phone with Corey almost immediately and was like, "Dude, we're back together. Does that offer still stand?" and he was like "Really?! Cool! Yeah, let's work on that!" That's really when Touch and Go came into the picture.

Keith: We had all the songs done by then, so we got together and practiced a lot.

Dan: Practice makes perfect, and we pretty much practiced constantly. If we had an hour to go out to Erik's mom's place and practice, we'd do it, because we could fit it in. More than anything else, though, we just wanted to do it. We loved playing together.

Erik: We were really into rehearsing. Hoisting amplifiers over our heads to go rehearse in an attic or play in my mom's basement. She'd sleep upstairs and just ask us to let her know when we were finished.

Keith: That's a big point that really needs to be emphasized—this band would not exist if it weren't for Ruth Tunison. That's where we practiced, and it was the only place we could consistently practice. She put up with that racket.

The band faced plenty of obstacles in their day-to-day. Just being able to play together was a challenge. What kept them going was their intense creative focus and work ethic. Their dedication to writing, rehearsing, and playing live as much as possible showed that they were dedicated to being a cut above any other band on the scene.

Boombox rehearsal recordings from this period made it onto a cassette only compilation called *Code Blue*, released by Sean Duffy and Patti Pezzati, the same people behind the *Last Rites* fanzine. "Live Wire" and "Fuck Ups" appear on here as early demos. Additionally, a ramped-up cover of Wire's "Champs" is arguably the highlight of the three songs that appear on the cassette, as the band makes the song their own, shaving nearly thirty seconds off the track's already-brief 1:28 runtime. Even at this faster tempo, one can very clearly hear how big of an influence Wire had on the band's overall sound.

Prepared as ever, with Rusk serving as producer, Die Kreuzen entered Detroit's Multi-Track Studios in early April to record what became their debut LP.

Keith: At the time, Corey was living in Dearborn, so he invited us to come up there to record and stay with him. We practiced for a little bit and then drove up to Dearborn. Corey drove us to the studio every day in his little car.

Dan: It seemed to take a while to get there, but everyone there [Metro Detroit] drove like maniacs. Corey was just all over the place. At that point there were still fiery wrecks all over Detroit—like, all these abandoned cars on fire.

Corey Rusk: It was a different time. It's relatively easy now to purchase a computer, some software, and microphones for a few thousand dollars, record yourself at home, and have it sound pretty good. Back then, the closest option to that was purchasing a four-track recorder, and even then the quality of recording wasn't the best. For us to be able to move up to a sixteen- or twenty-four-track studio, that was, like, such a massive jump in sound quality but also a significant jump in recording costs.

With that in mind, the recording budgets we had back then were minuscule to what you started to see ten to twenty years later. You had better be well rehearsed and really have your shit together, because every minute in the studio counted. There was no running behind schedule and staying in the studio for an additional week. You'd do long twelve-to-fifteen-hour days and just get it done, because there was no option for more time than what was available.

They soon began work on the album with engineer, Rick Canzano. Canzano's background and taste had little to do with the scene that Die

Kreuzen and Touch and Go belonged to, but his technical acumen, coupled with a willingness to work with them, was enough to get him the job.

Corey Rusk: I have to say, having worked in other studios with engineers who fit various stereotypes like hippie or whatnot, Rick was tolerant and cooperative, at least in my memory. We kept going back to that studio because it was a decent studio for the price, and at the time punk rock was not an accepted norm, and in general the people at the studio were very tolerant of us and what we wanted to do. For that time period, that was a big plus.

Rick Canzano (recording engineer, *Die Kreuzen*): I came from a jazz background and really wasn't into the punk and hardcore scene. It wasn't my musical preference, but I loved production, and I loved helping create art. I read everything I could get my hands on. I was totally into it at the time, and I had recorded a lot by the time we made that first album. My big thing was getting a really good drum sound—I loved doing that. I'm sure we had some reference records that Corey wanted me to listen to, but that was it.

Corey Rusk: I think every punk band at that time really just wanted to make a record that sounded as good as the Germs *GI* LP. That record was the ultimate balance between production and performance.

Rick Canzano: The goal was really just to capture the sound of the band on tape. We set up, got all the sounds in one night, and then came back the next day fresh and started cutting tracks. We did bass and drums live, reference guitar, and a scratch vocal. We didn't use a click track because we didn't need one; I remember thinking they were really tight.

Erik: We really played the hell out of those songs—we were really well rehearsed. But then it took a day to drive there and then some time to set up and whatever else, so it felt like we had a few days after this really intensive rehearsing, which I think brought a spontaneity to those recording sessions that was really really great. It made a huge difference.

Keith: We went in and pretty much blasted everything out in one or two takes for the most part. I think a lot of those songs were first takes, actually. We had been so well rehearsed with the songs by that point that we knew them pretty well. I think starting with getting drum sounds to the end of tracking vocals, it was probably no more than three days or so. We mixed it in a few days as well. We'd pretty much mix until our ears were fried. The tracking and mixing total was maybe five days at the most. I remember it going by very quickly.

Dan: They did a lot as a three-piece, and when they got a good bass-and-drum track then Brian would do guitars and Keith cleaned up some bass stuff if he needed to do that.

While the band's performances and songs did most of the heavy lifting, one must also acknowledge the album's unique and rather appropriate production. Rick Canzano was a notable step up from working with a student engineer. Canzano had technical chops and plenty of experience in studios, which made the band sound better than ever on record.

Brian: I was having a blast because that was the first recording studio that we had ever been in. The exhilaration of being able to record our stuff professionally was just a thrill. It was the best fucking feeling in the world.

Dan: It was a new thing to be in a nice proper studio, with thirty-six channels and all that.

Brian: We clashed a little bit with Rick about how things should sound, and it was kind of frustrating, but we got to where we needed it to be. At the time I didn't know anything about recording, but I always thought that the guitars on that record sounded kind of strange. It wasn't until later that I realized the microphones on my guitar amp were out of phase, and that's why they sound the way they do on that record, kind of hollow and boxy.

Rick Canzano: The guitar was hard for me to get a handle on because most of the time it was rhythm guitar, but it was so fast. The leads were little melodies that would flow in and out and it wasn't conventional. Even when he [Brian] took a solo, it was unlike anything I had heard at the time, so I couldn't even really judge them that way.

Keith: We knew exactly what we were doing, and I think that helped him out. We knew the songs really well by that point, so if there were mistakes, we knew there were mistakes. Corey being there definitely helped as well

Steve Albini: I took the impression that Corey was involved as sort of an intervening influence. Corey had done recording on his own and had spent enough time in studios and knew what a good punk record sounded like, so I wouldn't be surprised if Corey's influence played some role in the way that record was recorded. That's a crucial element, to have someone sympathetic and familiar in the control room, telling the engineer not to worry that there's too much distortion or that the person is hitting the cymbals too hard.

Corey Rusk: I don't remember the exact number of days, but I believe we recorded and mixed all the songs in, like, four days? Record time by today's standards! And even today that album still sounds great.

Dan: I remember Corey telling [his former wife] Lisa when we came back at the end of the day, "Yeah we're all proud of Dan; he knocked out all those songs today in, like, three hours." We were all just really happy. We were making progress, putting one big foot in front of the other. It couldn't have been more than four or five days, tops.

The last day, I did vocals, and we just burned through those twenty-one songs, all double-tracked. One or two of them are triple tracked. "All White" might have five or six vocal tracks on it. I just wanted to layer it up and have it sound super-crazy like that.

Corey Rusk: Looking back on it, across all of the punk scenes going on in the world, so many great records have stood the test of time. Even though they might be technically flawed, there's something about having to just go in there and do it, just pouring yourself into it in a very short amount of time and accepting it with all of its flaws. I think that process yielded these performances and recordings that could never be reproduced. If the band had three weeks in the studio and had the chance to overdub every little thing to perfection, it never would have captured the moment the way those forced short recording sessions did. The album marked the beginning of a band who was starting to find their own sound. Production was ramped up, the performances were much tighter, and as a result the album was a considerable jump forward not only for the band but for the scene overall. While *Cows and Beer* sounded like a band that was a part of a larger scene, by the time they reached their first album Die Kreuzen were sonically peerless. The eclecticism of their personal tastes was subtly beginning to come through in the music, making them sound like they were from an entirely different planet than most of their contemporaries.

Steve Albini: What's cool about them overall is that they each came up with something to hang their hat on. The bass is really brittle and rattly and has this sort of atypical sound to it, but you could imagine some kid deciding to play that way. Just hearing it and being completely invigorated by it and owning it—like, "Yeah, okay, this is how I'm gonna play, that's what I'm gonna sound like from here on out." Brian's guitar was really shrill and piercing, and he was playing this gnarly Kramer guitar that was notorious for being really spikey-sounding and unwieldy. But he owned it—like, "I'm gonna have this ferocious, really biting sound—this is mine and I'm going to own it." And then Dan has this approach that carries a lot of emotional intensity but no tune, and it's like he's the emotional center of the band—that's his role and he's happy there. He's not trying to get people to sing along. You can tell that each of them sort of solved the riddle of what they were going to do in the band independent of one another, and then stuck to it. The band as a whole was a synthesis of these things, these individual choices of how they were going to play and navigate it. I just loved the way that each of those individual riddles were solved in a way that made for a unique band at the end of the process.

That first record is such a great statement and example of that, because none of them were following a pattern, none of them were mimicking anybody. When you listen to the first record of most bands, my bands included, you can rattle off the things that they were imitating. You can spot the mimicry instantly. And there's just nothing about that Die Kreuzen record that sounds like it's received wisdom. It sounds like they dreamed all that shit up on their own. Like, no one would have ever been taught to play that way—you can only come up with those things on your own.

Perhaps the most notable shift in the band's sound came from Dan Kubinski, whose vocal style evolved from a shout to a full-on terrifying scream. Screaming in a musical setting had existed decades prior, but it was always used as a punctuation mark for added emphasis. With its roots in gospel and blues, it found its way into rock 'n' roll via acts like Little Richard, evolving as time progressed. Everyone from Janis Joplin and James Brown to Sly Stone and Tina Turner all employed the use of screaming as part of their vocal styles, but it was still used as a means of intensifying a moment or lyric.

The band's razor-sharp performances give the album both a focused precision and driving propulsion, but it's Kubinski's vocal performance that further pushes the album into a class all its own. While virtually all punk and hardcore vocalists of the day delivered their vocals in a yelling or shouting fashion, few had yet to truly push their voices even further into full-on screaming. Bad Brains' vocalist HR had a distinct and bratty yelp that was equal parts melodic and snot-nosed, but aside from a small handful

of acts at the time (see releases from Negative Approach, Void, Siege, and Terveet Kädet, and the first Meat Puppets EP for further examples) Kubinski's vocals on the self-titled album are among the earliest recorded documents of screaming in hardcore punk. One can hear the beginnings of him finding this style on the band's 1982 demo, specifically on tracks like "No Name" and "Don't Say Please." This was a conscious decision on Kubinski's part, and the result suits the music perfectly, sharpening the album's already jagged edge.

Brian: Dan used his voice as an instrument, which was outside of the norm at the time.

Corey Rusk: I thought Dan had a really unique and amazing voice. I remember his vocal approach fitting in so well with the music. Every member of Die Kreuzen was doing something that was complementary to the whole in a way that wasn't always true of some of the bands back then. Void sounded crazed and frantic, but they seemed completely unhinged and out of control; Die Kreuzen seemed like they had focused their effort on executing a very specific thing.

I wouldn't liken their vocal styles to sounding anything like each other, but John Brannon was blowing his voice out in a similar manner. If you listen to those Negative Approach records, it sounds like his voice is going to get ripped to shreds any second.

Thurston Moore: I just always thought that that was Dan's range. In a way, you could actually hear that sort of banshee-esque voice within the music, because the music was so loud and fast that it cut through. I almost thought it was like a strategy for him [laughs]. He wasn't really conforming to whatever standards were happening in hardcore at the time. The band was just sort of setting themselves apart immediately. They were hardcore by default, but they were something else entirely. Dan's whole demeanor was different, with the long hair and all that stuff; he was just a different kind of figure.

Paul Mahern: I remember being really struck by Dan's vocal style. I just recall thinking, "Wow, he's gonna hurt his voice!" because it was a real shift. I kinda wondered, "Did they record this when he wasn't feeling well?" It was a big shift in his style.

David Pajo: Hardcore bands just weren't doubling their vocals. You barely had time to get your songs recorded back then.

Dennis Lyxzen (singer, Refused, International Noise Conspiracy, Fake Names): It doesn't sound like anything from that time really, maybe a little bit like Bad Brains or Dead Kennedys, but really, his singing was just so different.

Brad Wood: That scream was just so unique. Dan was doing something vocally that I hadn't heard anyone else do full-time. He was literally decades ahead of everyone else.

Steve Albini: Those vocals sounded to me like they came as a result of the music. Like, if you're making music that sounds like that, where it isn't super-melodic or tuneful, it makes sense to project this sort of personal horror all the time by just screaming and shrieking. By default, punk rock wasn't an institutional thing—you had to do it yourself. If you're doing it yourself then you're going to come up with your own solutions to the problems that you'll face.

Dan: I think Corey actually suggested that I double-track my voice. At first, I was just kind of like, "Really?" He used the Minor Threat records as a reference point for that sort of thing, and so the first time around I just sort of did it to humor him, but after hearing it I immediately was impressed by how much fuller it sounded. There were a couple tracks like "All White" where there were more than two vocal tracks on there. They just seemed to call for a little more power. "All White" might have five or six vocal tracks on it. I just wanted to layer it up and have it sound super-crazy like that.

Kubinski's vocals perfectly suited both the sound of the album and his lyrics. The self-titled album was the last time that the band included a lyric sheet with the album, and review of the lyrics shows exactly what Kubinski spoke of previously—choosing to focus on the personal rather than the political. Many of the song lyrics deal with his own personal struggles with others and the growing pains of young adulthood. A handful of tracks, most notably "Dirt and Decay," choose to look outward rather than inward, touching on topics like poverty and wealth inequality. Die Kreuzen was never an outspoken political band, but Kubinski's references to the social climate of the world around him showed that he was able to look beyond himself with concern and compassion. Whether singing about his conflicts with personal relationships or the class struggle of others, Kubinski's lyrics express a general frustration and hopelessness of life during the Reagan era without once ever mentioning the man's name.

The new material wasn't only more aggressive vocally; the music itself was darker, meaner, and noisier as well. The studio upgrade allowed the band to make music that was sonically better than what they had done before, but the band's equipment played an equally important role in the overall sound of the album. Tools are what you make of them, and when you have no choice but to use what is at your disposal you are forced to make the most of your resources. In the case of Die Kreuzen, the album's signature guitar feedback was born out of a design flaw in Egeness's guitar.

Brian: The Kramer guitar I played at the time was notorious for being really prone to feedback, way more than other guitars. I think it's because they didn't have enough wax around the pickups. Eventually, I just got fed up and decided to stop trying to fight it and instead started to incorporate it into what we were doing. It was just me feeding the guitar into certain parts of the speakers. I found that if I ran towards the speakers that I'd get this swirling kind of feedback, so that's what you hear on that record.

The sheets of guitar feedback flowing throughout the album only increased the sense of tension and dissonance. Once mixed, the tracks were at times treated with a generous amount of reverb. For a different band playing another batch of songs, this wouldn't have made much of a difference, but in the case of *Die Kreuzen*, this stylistic choice helped give the album a sense of mood and atmosphere that wouldn't exist without it. It''s similar to the way that reverb is used on Joy Division's 1979 debut LP *Unknown Pleasures;* it creates a distance while also subtly amplifying things on the tracks that would otherwise go unheard. Panning delays and reverbs give the vocals an eerie distance that predates the now-distinct stylistic decisions made by many Scandinavian black metal acts in the late '80s and '90s. It's this quality—alongside all the others previously mentioned—that makes the album sound as unique as it does. While *Cows and Beer* sounded like young adults making music as part of the American hardcore movement, Die Kreuzen possessed an almost otherworldly sound, a quality that it still maintains over thirty years later.

The first Die Kreuzen album is rooted in hardcore, but with dark undertones that create a tense and moody atmosphere, sharing as much sonic DNA with albums like *Porcupines* as it does with *Group Sex*.

Paul Mahern: I would say that the real difference for me as far as Midwestern bands go is that they had more of a post-punk approach, especially in the guitar playing. It reminded me more of bands like the

Fall or even Crass. They were much more adventurous musically than a lot of their contemporaries. It seems like a lot of the bands around them were simpler in their approach, taking influence from more straight-ahead punk rock. Die Kreuzen always struck me as an art band. Like, from the start, they just really stood out as being different from all the other bands.

Visually, the album's graphics and layout were handled by their manager, Richard Kohl. While Richard didn't have a reference cassette of the music to hear while crafting the layout, by this point he was more than familiar with their repertoire and quickly got to work on the album's sleeve. His recent relocation to San Francisco provided him with plenty of places to explore, and the album art was directly influenced by his surroundings.

Richard Kohl: I had spent a lot of time roaming around San Francisco, and I was just fascinated by it. I'd go to some of the more industrial areas in town, and under freeway overpasses and stuff you'd see these posters. They were these ads for machine performances from Survival Research Laboratories. They'd put up these posters for these events, and on them they'd have photos of these machines that would basically tear each other apart—shoot flames or bowling balls or whatever. A lot of industry was leaving San Francisco, so all these factories were vacant or padlocked or whatever. People would go into these buildings and steal all this equipment, reconfiguring it to their needs, adding scraps from dead animals that they'd find, just to make these machines look organic. I saw some of that and thought it was incredible and became really inspired by that. When you look at the album sleeve, that's really what I was drawing inspiration from. I remember hearing someone once describe the drawing as cockroaches? They're not cockroaches—they're more like dogs.

I used to go to these art-supply stores and buy the cheapest stuff they had. The cheaper it was, the better for me—stuff you'd find in the bargain bin and whatnot. The lettering I used was kinda damaged, and some of it didn't really transfer right, but I liked that about it. I'd often use a Xerox machine to blow up the type and also as a way to distort it a little bit more. All the text was done that way using transfer letters.

Dan: We'd tell Richard that we'd need something and then suddenly it would just arrive. For that first album I just remember getting that in the mail in, like, a thin envelope and the only thing protecting it was a thin sheet of rice paper. We unwrapped it and there it was, all done.

Richard Kohl's illustration for *Die Kreuzen* was born of wandering around industrial areas in San Francisco.

One of the many photos shot to promote the band's debut full-length, c. 1984. Photo: Corey Rusk.

Keith: We never saw much of anything until Richard gave it to us, and it would always be great and fit perfectly with the music.

Kim Thayil: That Richard Kohl album cover? Fucking amazing! Had I thought about it more back then, I probably would have asked him to do something for one of the Soundgarden records.

David Pajo: That album cover is a world you entered. Some weird tortured hellscape, like a ring of Dante's Inferno. It's scary and shadowy and dank down there.

The album has a mystique and unknown quality that's often missing today. Nowadays, every band has a Wikipedia page or something, and you can learn everything you want. If you had that first Die Kreuzen album, that might be all you really knew about them. You had the music and the amazing cover and insert art. It was you and your brain processing the sound and visuals to fanaticize about anything, everything involving the band, because all you had was what they gave you. That's how bands become mythic.

Debut albums often have little expectation to live up to but, since the band had released *Cows and Beer* and a handful of demo cassettes prior to their debut LP, listeners had a better frame of reference as to what to expect of it. Even so, it's difficult to say if anyone was prepared for it. Drawing on tracks from their previous releases as well as over a dozen new ones, Die Kreuzen's self-titled debut finds the band at its most vicious and unrelenting, delivering twenty-one tracks in less than a half-hour. It's a hardcore punk album in the most ideal sense of the term, and anyone attempting to do the same can only aspire to the standard it set.

The album opens up with "Rumors," one of the album's slowest songs. Though a soft open, it still manages to introduce many of the album's major elements—the metronome-tight rhythm section of Brammer and Tunison, Egeness's swirling guitar feedback, and Kubinski's distinctive vocals. Listen closely and before the song's first note you can hear a split second of Erik Tunison's drumstick clicks as he counts the song in. It may have been a difficult thing to edit out, especially during the days of splicing two-inch tape, but this artifact being left in is a subtle reminder of how the album was made—just four guys in a room playing through their songs.

"Rumors" may not immediately highlight the band's speed and precision, but it's not long before it gives way to "This Hope," a fast and trashy offering that's more in the vein of the tracks on *Cows and Beer*. The upgraded production and tighter performances, coupled with the band members' continually growing skills, make it seem quite far from that release, though. "This Hope" makes it very clear that Die Kreuzen are masters of their craft, combining speed, aggression, and precision in a way that few if anyone else could at the time.

Re-recording songs from previous releases can be risky; listeners grow attached to specific versions and have difficulty adjusting to updated ones. Some of *Die Kreuzen*'s songs were nearly four years old by the time they were recorded for the album, and the performances captured on tape possess a specific energy brought on by the band's overall confidence and comfort with having played the songs extensively. As a result, every re-recorded song on the self-titled debut eclipses any previous iterations, firmly cementing these as the definitive versions.

The self-titled album's mood and atmosphere is present throughout a majority of the album's twenty-one tracks, but it arguably shines brightest on "All White." When a previous version of the song appeared on the band's demo cassette and on the Master Tape compilation, it was drier and more stripped down, with few enhancements. The song was still a favorite of the band's live sets, with the audience participating in the choruses, but when the time came for the band to record their debut album, "All White" was one of the band's older tracks that, once done over, went from good to great.

The most noticeable difference with the album version can be heard in Dan Kubinski's vocal approach. On the demo cassette and Master Tape versions, Kubinski's delivery is more in line with John Lydon or Darby Crash—snottier and more antagonistic than anything else. The album version highlights Kubinski's signature scream to fine effect, the lyrics amplified by his intensely agonized delivery. The repeated "white" choruses are replaced with drawn out pained screams, enhanced by the reverb that allows it to echo throughout the mix. The performances and execution of "All White" make it what it is, claustrophobic, tortured, and like little else that was on a hardcore punk record at the time.

Kim Thayil: "All White" was the song that everyone agreed that there was just something else going on with this band. It had this psychedelic element to it, a definitely trippiness and dark quality.

Lou Barlow: Die Kreuzen predated a lot of that slower hardcore thing with "All White." It was kinda like [Black Flag's] "Damaged," but it eventually got faster, too. It was just different—they really did seem ahead of their time, like right away. The guitar playing was so fucking good—like, instantly I was like, "Holy shit, this guy is a shredder," but not like a heavy-metal shredder. It felt much more informed by post-punk.

Most of the album's tracks fall into the uber-fast sub-200bpm range, but its slower moments are just as memorable. "In School," from the band's demo as well as *Cows and Beer*, sounds tighter and leaner on all accounts. "Mannequin," arguably the album's most straightforward and simple track, remains engaging and distinct, with Egeness's Robert-Fripp-meets-Greg-Ginn guitar approach being the song's main highlight.

The album features plenty of standout performances from each member. Whether its Brammer's intensely precise tremolo picking on the intros of more than a handful of songs ("No Time" being an especially impressive one), Tunison's ability to start, stop and start again on a moment's notice, Egeness's ability to weave in and out of the arrangements without ever falling out of time, or Kubinski's unrelenting vocal agony, there are few albums from hardcore's first wave that sound this focused and have this strong a sense of self.

Cows and Beer was a document of a young band finding its voice in the greater landscape of American hardcore, but it also had common ground with many other acts of the era. It was the last time that one could hear the record and possibly be uncertain as to who the artist was. The self-titled debut is a document of a band who had found their sonic identity, and while this sound evolved over the course of their career, Die Kreuzen had now developed a sound that was entirely their own.

Corey Rusk: When we finished that first record, I just remember thinking, "This is one of the best things ever." I was certainly hoping and maybe even expecting that other people would feel the same way. It seemed inconceivable to me that anyone could dislike that record. At the same time, I also knew that you could be so sure of it but have it end up not succeeding. I'm interested in what I'm interested in, and I want to be involved with it, regardless of whether it will sell or not.

Brian: I remember when we got the actual records I just called everyone I knew. I was so excited to have a full-length record of my music. It was the most amazing thing I had ever seen—we were on a fucking *album*.

Dan: We were so proud of that thing, man. I had a cassette dub, and I remember playing it for some of the Tar Babies and Mecht Mench guys in the van. They were digging it. They loved the way it sounded.

Rick Canzano: I gotta say—I'm really happy with the way that it sounds. I think it's aged really well and still sounds great.

Upon its release, *Die Kreuzen* received a considerable amount of positive press, and word began to spread about the album. Though several fanzines reviewed the album favorably, one review stands out from the lot. The July 1984 issue of *Maximum Rocknroll* ran a review of the album by Tim Yohannan that simply read, "This is fucking great!" repeated twelve times, with no other information about the band, album or otherwise. Though it said very little, it was enough to pique the interest of more than a few readers and to this day remains an important part of both the band's and album's legacy.

Mike Gitter (founder, *xXx Fanzine;* Vice President A&R, Century Media): The first time I heard of them was reading that "This is fucking great! This is fucking great!" *Maximum Rocknroll* review, and I just kinda read that and thought, "Yeah . . . you know, chances are this record is gonna be fucking great."

Janet Billig Rich (A&R and publicity, Caroline Records): That would have brought me to it, because I read *Maximum Rocknroll* religiously. That's how I found out about anything at that time, and I'm sure that was the same for a lot of other people as well. If Tim Yohannon told me to buy anything I'd get it blind—I'd just feel confident that it was going to be something good.

Thurston Moore: Every once in a while there's a band that hits this galvanized spot where, to me, they become the greatest band . . . not even in America, but in the world . . . they just completely rule; they're white hot. I remember seeing this band called the Bush Tetras in, like, 1979 and they were new and they just hit this point where everyone in New York was going to see them. As far as I was concerned at that time, this was the greatest band in the world and I'm here watching them.

That *Maximum Rocknroll* review, that's exactly how I felt about Die Kreuzen. Right when they put out that first album, Die Kreuzen were just incinerating everyone around them with what they were doing. It was hardcore, but it was something else. It really was white-hot. It was its own

DIE KREUZEN - "Die Kreuzen" LP

This is fucking great! This is fucking great! This is fucking great! This is fucking great! This is fucking great! This is fucking great! This is fucking great! This is fucking great! This is fucking great! This is fucking great! This is fucking great! This is fucking great! (TY)
(Touch & Go--P.O. Box 716--Maumee, OH 43537)

Above: Review of the first Die Kreuzen album by Tim Yohannan in Issue 15 (July 1984) of *Maximum RocknRoll.*

Below: Touch and Go advertisement for first Die Kreuzen album in Issue 15 (July 1984) of *Maximum RockandRoll.*

thing—it wasn't just hardcore or punk or noise, it was Die Kreuzen. For a moment there, they were the best, they were the shit. There was no contest.

Steve Albini: That album is still unique. Most of the other hardcore bands were pretty formulaic, but Die Kreuzen seemed to be drawing from a deeper well, and they were also more rabid than those other bands. Very few hardcore records could evoke genuine terror. They were terrific musicians, which meant they could execute things with precision that other bands just blurred over. They stood out instantly. Great, aggressive recording as well.

Mike Gitter: When I heard that first record, it was not like anything I had ever heard before because it was so . . . it had this sense of musicality that was rare and distinct. They didn't sound like a band from any scene or musical tradition; they were writing their own rules and sounds and ideas from song to song. When I got it, it was just breathtaking and brain-scarring. Dan's voice goes beyond rage, really. There's so much soul, sorrow, and emotion when he opens his mouth. We had never heard anyone sing like that before.

Steve Albini: The drawing on the album cover is engrossing because you can't really figure out what you're looking at. There was a slightly cryptic quality to it. And that gave you the initial hint that this band was taking themselves seriously, that it wasn't just a goof.

When you listen to the music, it was expertly played. Music at that pace is often a mess. In some cases that aesthetic is fine because you don't feel like they're trying to tell you anything. It just feels like someone who's just playing. With that album, there's this very strong emotional content. Dan had this sort of personalized frustrated sound as opposed to this projected rage. *That* I could identify with.

It reminded me of the Bad Brains in the fact that music was so well articulated, and the parts were so well defined. It wasn't just "play fast,"—it was "play this very precise thing, at this specific intensity and then blow it up in a very precise way." You just got the impression that they were taking it seriously and that there was content there. It wasn't just an attitude in show business.

Mike Gitter: Bands like Die Kreuzen, Jerry's Kids, Siege, and Void, they just had this tortured suburban soul and this musical ambition that was bigger, broader, and more expansive than a lot of the bands in hardcore. Die Kreuzen were one of those bands that brought you into their world. Their name was different, their graphics were different. It was darker and gothier, more atmospheric. Sonically, they just brought it to a whole different world, and you can hear the beginning of that on that first record.

There are musical things in that record that have latched on in my mind and never let go. Like the bassline in "Rumors"? What the fuck is that? Like, even how the record opens—it's just explosive and it was such a complete "what the fuck is this?" In some ways it's technical; to this day there's nothing that sounds anything like it.

Bob Nastanovich (member, Pavement, Silver Jews): I had that first record and I thought it was great. It's just definitive punk rock in that it was just good, no-frills American hardcore. It wasn't like those English bands or anything, and it wasn't really like SST either. They were isolated in the Midwest, which is probably why they were doing their own thing.

Dennis Lyxzen: That first LP is really chaotic, like free jazz hardcore or something. The first time I put that record on, I just remember thinking, "What the hell is going on here?" There's so many songs on this record and it just sounds fucking insane. I remember thinking distinctly that this was just this crazy-sounding record, and the artwork and photos, it was just so wild. It kind of reminded me of Void because it had this otherworldly insanity, and what's not to love about that when you're nineteen years old, right? It was just like, "Oh shit, this is great."

Thurston Moore: I kept hearing about how Hüsker Dü was this really fast band, and I remember thinking I wanted to hear them because I wanted to hear the fastest band out there. Then they put out *Land Speed Record*, and I was disappointed that they actually really weren't. In a way, Die Kreuzen were fantastic because they were the fastest. They kind of won the speed trial there [laughs].

John Reis (member, Drive Like Jehu, Rocket from the Crypt, Hot Snakes): My friend Ian had this skateboard where he had screened the image of the first Die Kreuzen album cover onto it. It looked so cool, I thought it was made by some skate company, but he told me that he did it himself and that it was from a record cover. We went back to his house and he played it for me and it just blew me away.

We both kept referring to the "creepy crawl" element that it shared with Black Flag. Much like the first time that I heard Black Flag, it felt like we were kinda doing something a little bit wrong by listening to it. I had heard a couple of punk records by this point, so it wasn't like we had no reference point, but what they were doing was totally different from what everyone else was doing. In terms of hardcore, it had that sort of Discharge blasting quality, just a full-on attack. Some of the songs are these short little haikus. At that point, I had been playing guitar a little bit, and the guitar playing was so cool and innovative, in the same way that East Bay Ray and Greg Ginn were.

That Die Kreuzen record, though—by that point, a lot of bands had started to abandon that very literal type of intensity. That sinister kind of aggression that was very literal. There was nothing about that record that was subtle; it's just so intense and creepy. It felt like we were playing with a Ouija board or something ... just like, "Damn, this is some really dark shit" [laughs]. My friend and I, we would play that record and just trash the fuckin' house. I would jump up and down on my bed—it was just this conduit, this lightning rod where the music would just energize everyone.

Greg Anderson (member, Sunn O))), Goatsnake; co-founder, Southern Lord Records): By 1984, I was really into underground metal. Metallica, Venom, Slayer, Mötörhead—all that. There was this hardcore band from [Seattle] called False Liberty that kinda turned me onto this whole new world of music. Among that was the first Die Kreuzen record, and it just blew my mind how fast and aggressive it was. I was around fifteen, so I didn't completely understand the technicalities of playing music. It took me years later to realize the genius of Die Kreuzen and how crazy those songs were in their structures and arrangements. Everything was so advanced and different from everything else. The reason that band stands up is because they were such great musicians—they were on a whole different planet. There was such a formula for hardcore, and a lot of bands followed that and did well, but Die Kreuzen created their own formula that they followed. It had elements of punk and hardcore, but they created something that was entirely their own.

Plenty of punk and hardcore records from the '80s sound horrible, but there's a certain quality about them where the passion and intensity of the players still comes through. Back then, you just kinda had to accept things as how they were; it was the best that you could do, and you just had to kinda live with it. In a lot of ways, no one really knew what they were doing. That Die Kreuzen record, though, that record sounded like they totally knew what they were doing. It almost sounds fragile to me, like it's going to break at any moment.

A lot of early-'80s hardcore records, you can predict a lot of things about them. You can tell what bands they were influenced by—you could probably tell where the songs were going to go. With that record, all of those things just flew out the window. To this day, it's just a mind-blowing record.

Justin Trosper (guitarist and vocalist, Unwound): That first album, for all of its really fast punk kinda qualities, it's still super-weird. You hear the demos for a lot of those songs and they're great, but by the time that first record comes around it's just something else entirely. It was so evolved—it was beyond the Hüsker Dü records. In terms of punk, very few records were that good on a technical level. There are things on that record that just aren't on a lot of punk records, just the musicianship alone. The guitars are really complex, the drumming is super-tight and fast, his vocals are totally next-level. They're doing things as a band that most people weren't capable of. They were still playing punk but with this sort of thrash-metal level of proficiency.

Kim Thayil: That first album is so memorable for me. Brian did that insane stutter-stop kinda thing on guitar that almost made it sound like the record was skipping. He did that in a few songs, and he did it really fast. Not only did it live up to the guys in Mr. Epp's claim [that they were among the fastest bands in hardcore] but that stutter-stop was just so tight, and I'm sure it was accented by Keith and Erik. It was just amazing.

They were this cool hardcore band with great guitar and bass sounds—like, they played with choruses and reverbs and delays. Chorus specifically was more so used by a lot of the British New Romantic bands, or like early U2. The first time I heard that kind of guitar sound on a hardcore record was that first Die Kreuzen record. They used these interesting kinds of effects that you didn't hear on records like that, but they were still playing hardcore. It was fast and streamlined and electric; it felt like it was from the future.

Matt Sweeney (member, Chavez, Zwan, Hard Quartet): These guys were clearly very much into music before they heard punk. I feel like the role that punk played with them had less to do with playing and more to do with putting out a record. I think that was the difference: it was less about being a guide on how to play and more about the ability to make your own music and know that you could put it out and play shows. There's a huge distinction between that versus the default hardcore style. Die Kreuzen was pulling influence from so many more places, but the fact that they were doing that and then focusing all of that into their own take on hardcore? *That's* what made them so cool.

***Die Kreuzen* stands as one of the best hardcore albums ever committed to tape, still sounding as fresh and vital as it did forty-plus years ago. At the time of its release, word began to spread about this band from Milwaukee who were heavier and faster than the average hardcore band. The album was complete, their legend beginning to grow. The hard work of writing, recording, and releasing a stellar album was over; now they had to go out there and promote it.**

With a full-length album completed, the band was ready to get back on the road. Their previous experiences helped them acclimate to touring life, and the critical acclaim of the first album helped the band expand their reach to places they had yet to play. Being in a touring band is never an easy life, though, and to dedicate the amount of time necessary to it the four members had to work wherever they could.

Keith: We went out and played while we were waiting for that record to come out. We didn't play around here [Milwaukee] that much at that time. That was the first time we went out east. At that time none of us held down what would be considered a "good" job. We were working at Pizza Man, and even though we'd technically leave when we'd go out on tour, they'd be so busy and desperate for people by the time we came back from tour that they'd give us our jobs back. We'd always try to be considerate about it and give them enough notice. After a while they started to figure out that we were all in the same band.

Erik: There was a short period of time when all of us were working at Pizza Man, including the guy who was doing sound for us on tour. It was very insular.

Brian: We all had the same goal, so living and working and playing together wasn't really an issue.

Dan: We'd leave to go on tour and just be like, "See ya," and head out [laughs]. We somehow managed to be there off and on for a few years.

Above: The band tear up a record store basement in support of their debut LP, c. 1984. Photo courtesy of Die Kreuzen. Photographer unknown.

Below: Erik and the band's homemade T-shirts hanging out to dry at Corey and Lisa Rusk's home in 1984. Photo courtesy of Die Kreuzen.

We had a friend there named Tom who was also a manager at one point, and he'd let us go out pretty much whenever we wanted to with no hassle.

Erik: Eventually I started working for a company that installed security systems. I sat in a bunker and waited for different alarms to come in. They had some older alarms that worked on ticker tape. They were just starting to computerize around then.

The positive reception of the band's debut full length built on the foundation laid down by *Cows and Beer* and the moderate touring the band had done by that point. Not wanting to lose momentum, the band set out to hit the road in support of the full length.

Dan: We always had the plan to extend our range further when touring. We'd add a few cities every tour, striking out further each time. We'd do portions of it and then come home.

Keith: We'd do weekends and then make it back for the beginning of the week. For the most part we started to plan it where we'd be gone for three weeks at a time.

Dan: We'd do as many weekends as we could around the Midwest and then make it back. Occasionally we'd do shorter week-long things. For the most part we'd plan them out to where we'd be out for at least three weeks at a time. Three weeks was just enough to make ends meet and go places and get a good bellyful, but also enough to where it was right around the time when we'd want to come back home.

Keith: Erik got our first proper van from this place he was working at called Central Control.

Erik: The company I was working for at the time sold us a van for, like, $400. I think it had 100,000 miles on it. They made us paint over the logo of the company, but we left "Emergency Services" on the side, which I'm pretty sure helped us park illegally a few times. After the rust built up quite a bit, though, I think it became pretty apparent that we weren't actually from a company [laughs].

Keith: The first couple times we bought Ford Econolines. This one time we went into kind of a sketchy area to buy one, and when we asked the guy how much he wanted for it, he just said, "You got any guns? Guns are as good as money."

Dan: There was never money for a hotel room in the early days. Hotels were out of the question, so we'd usually end up staying at someone's house or, if we had a little money, staying at campgrounds. For about $20 you could stay at a campsite with bathrooms, showers, and electricity.

Keith: That was always fun. Erik had a little two-burner propane stove that we would use.

Erik: I had a good number of experiences with camping from when I was younger. I knew from going around the countryside with my family that staying at state campgrounds was a good place to kill a day for cheap. We'd sleep in the van or on top of the van if the weather was okay. We'd bring along some cookware and a gas cooker and cook for ourselves. I have some really good memories from those times. Not too bad for five bucks!

Keith: It's way different than how it is now where you can eat out all the time and tour in a huge van or something. We had, like, what? a dollar a day for food?

Erik: It took a while for us to start paying out a per-diem for each of us.

Keith: We'd get stuff like bologna and bread.

Erik: Cook up some beans and weenies on the gas cookstove on the dumpster behind the club.

When not camping, though, the band stayed with friends or anyone who would put them up for a night. Sometimes, though, the unorthodox place to stay ended up being better in theory than in practice. While on tour in 1985, a car accident found them stuck in Baltimore for a few days while waiting for their van to get fixed.

Keith: We got rear ended and were stopped because of construction. This guy comes up driving this huge old Pontiac or something, obviously not paying attention and just slams into the poor little sports car behind us, just accordion-ing that thing. I forget who was in back, but I was sitting there and all of a sudden I just feel the impact and one of our Anvil briefcases rocketed from the back of the van and hit me in the head. I probably had some sort of minor concussion or whatever, and this girl in the car that hit us just looked at me and says "Yeah, you might not wanna go to sleep because you might not wake up" and I'm just like "Get the hell away from me you hillbilly".

Above: Drivin n Cryin's Kevn Kinney camps with Die Kreuzen, c. 1987. Photo courtesy of Die Kreuzen.

Below: A common sight during the band's tenure, the beloved $5 campsite, c. 1987. Photo courtesy of Die Kreuzen.

Erik: I know we were on our way to Richmond VA when it happened. We got rear ended, and it damaged the engine, but we didn't know it for several hours to a day [later]. What transpired is that since we had it in gear, it fried the transmission.

Keith: We were playing in Baltimore with Tales of Terror and I think Battalion of Saints. This place was like an abandoned storefront that they had built a stage in. The guy running the show was kind of weird and had this bad reputation for inviting young men to stay at his apartment and whatnot, so we decided to sleep in the venue instead. We were always prepared for that outcome, so we had sleeping bags and all that.

He locked us in the club because it wasn't exactly in the safest area. We were about to go to sleep and then we heard someone trying to break in, but they left once they heard us in there or something. We woke up again about a half hour later and heard all this rustling. The place was trashed—people had left McDonald's bags and beer cans and all kinds of stuff just littered around the club. And then I woke up and I felt this weird heavy thing on my leg in my sleeping bag. And I'm like, "Wait ... rustling on the floor? Something big on my leg?" and immediately realized it was a rat. I smacked the thing off my leg and the thing went flying about twenty feet. The whole place was infested with them.

Dan: I can't remember what happened. I don't remember how we got out of there. I think we got off the floor and ended up sleeping on the stage?

Keith: I think I ended up sleeping on the stage, but needless to say I didn't get much rest that night.

Erik: Yeah, I think I somehow slept through that [laughs].

Keith: We ended up staying there for, like, three days, hanging out with the Tales of Terror guys. They would just get up and start drinking. First thing in the morning, no coffee, just crack open a bottle of whiskey and get some beers going. Man, they were a great band, though. Ferociously good, and they could still play when they were completely smashed.

The unpredictable nature of touring was to be expected, and ultimately, the goal was to play their personal best at each show and leave an impression on audiences. Videos from this period show a band that knew their songs

inside and out, and live sets were short blasts of sound, going from one song to the next. It's not dissimilar to the live approach of the Ramones: wasting no time and just going for the gusto every night.

David Pajo: They had played in Indiana in 1984. I wasn't at the show but my bandmates in Maurice were. There weren't that many punks in Louisville at the time, but everyone who was there from Louisville became a Die Kreuzen fan that night. Apparently, they totally stole the show; like, from the second it started it went from a bunch of normal Midwestern folks just standing around to just complete apocalypse [laughs]. The way people spoke about them, it was like they hit the first note and the roof caved in.

All the punk girls were in love with them—everyone just loved their look and the way they performed. I kept hearing so much about Keith from my band—they kept saying, "The bass player does this thing, it's not quite headbanging, it's this different thing he does." They kept referring to it as like this "rubber-band spine" move, because he'd bend back super far with all this hair and then he'd lash forward really fast. It was like this single emotional headbang that would just happen.

After that show, all those girls started dressing like Keith! They started to hairspray their hair and wear those kinda baggy white shirts with the tight denim. All the ladies fell for it! Their punk rock boyfriends were totally not into it [laughs].

At that time, there was divide in what you were into back then. There were the goths and then there were the hardcore kids, and there wasn't much overlap between the two. That makes me like them even more, honestly. At the height of the whole hardcore thing, Keith had the balls to show up in that world with that kinda look. He was so good at going against the grain, which to me is the most punk rock thing to do. Just totally going the opposite way as all those purists. People are way too uptight, man.

Neko Case (solo artist, member, New Pornographers): When you're young you don't separate fashion from music at all, and man, Die Kreuzen had *the best* fuckin' hair.

Brad Wood: I saw Die Kreuzen on Halloween 1984 at the Cabaret Metro in Chicago. I remember being just as confused by their long hair as I was when I saw Black Flag. We had come in halfway through their set and figured there was another band playing before Die Kreuzen because they looked so different from the last time I had seen them. Eventually, towards the end of their set, Dan said, "Hey, thanks for coming out, we're Die Kreuzen from Milwaukee," and we were all like, "Holy shit!" They looked so different, and the music had definitely evolved—it just blew our minds. We talked about it the whole drive home.

Matt Sweeney: I remember seeing them at CBGB and my friends and I were such fans of theirs. There's this pizza place called St. Mark's Pizza that we used to go to all the time. I remember seeing Keith there once and we all freaked out—"Holy shit, it's the Die Kreuzen dude at St. Mark's Pizza, oh my fuckin' god!!"

Jon Wurster (drummer, Superchunk, Bob Mould): I had a band in Philadelphia called Psychotic Norman, and we played with Die Kreuzen in September of 1985. It was a basement of a house called the Crypt. I remember pulling up to the house and seeing their huge bread truck parked in front of there. I remember them sitting on the back porch and they just looked like these aliens. They looked very different from a lot of the bands that were part of the punk and hardcore scene. I just thought they looked amazing—they had this long hair and they all wore these cool clothes. Keith wore these cool paisley shirts and a suit jacket. They just looked fabulous. To me they just looked like they were part of the Paisley Underground scene.

I don't remember much about the actual show because you couldn't really see them and the sound wasn't the best. I remember pretty much just hearing bass. A friend of mine said to me as we were leaving, "Hey, man, I like bass as much as the next guy, but . . ."

It was around this time that they first met Sonic Youth, the New York four-piece whose groundbreaking and unorthodox approach to guitar playing was reinventing the idea of what a rock band could be. By this point, the former Crucifucks drummer Steve Shelley was now behind the kit. Die Kreuzen's initial introduction to Sonic Youth laid the foundation for a kinship that lasted for years to come, despite its somewhat less than ideal circumstances.

Keith: Sonic Youth traveled in a station wagon I'm pretty sure. Lee, Thurston, and Kim had a ton of guitars just kinda stacked on each other, pretty much none of them in cases. No drums either, just guitars and maybe

Above: Ramones fans for life, the band poses outside of CBGB in New York after a gig, c. 1986. Photo courtesy of Die Kreuzen. Photographer unknown.

Below: Die Kreuzen around the time of their debut album's release, c. 1984. Photo: Corey Rusk.

a few amps. I remember them borrowing our drums and guitar amps.

We went out with Steve Shelley to get Mexican food, and I remember someone coming in right as we got our food saying, "Steve, you're on in five minutes!" so he just scarfed his food down way too fast, and we all rushed back to the venue. During the set, Steve just kinda disappeared behind the drums every now and then to puke. There's footage of the show, and you can see it on the video! Still, they were great that night, and that started a relationship with them that continued for the rest of our career.

The places they played with, bands they played with, and people they stayed with all shaped their musical tastes. The band was always interested in hearing new music and playing in an active touring band ensured that they were exposed to plenty of it.

Dan: When we stayed with people, Keith and I would comb through their record collections and make tapes for the van. New albums, compilation tapes—just whatever. We got into a lot of new music through doing that.

Keith: I couldn't afford to buy a whole lot of records at the time. I didn't have a turntable, so I was a big cassette guy. They were portable and fairly inexpensive and durable. We had this big brown plastic case filled with tapes that we played in the van.

The process of absorbing new influences, coupled with playing approximately 100 shows in 1984 and 1985, made the band tighter while broadening their sonic language. Slowly, a handful of new songs began to appear in their sets around this time, with the band using live shows as a way to practice the new material. Eventually, the time came for the band to start thinking about making a new record.

Keith: I think we always just thought, "Wow, it would be really nice to be able to support ourselves with this," but we weren't willing to change at all. We wanted to be able to do what we did on our own terms. Part of it was that we took so long to write songs. We came from the '60s where people were releasing two records a year, and with the hardcore bands they'd release a bunch of stuff too. Either they were really prolific, or they had no filter and released everything. Our big thing was that we were never going to repeat ourselves. It was a couple of years between records at least, which at the time was enormous because it seemed like everyone was releasing stuff much more quickly.

Dan: I remember sitting on the roof of Corey's house in Detroit at the time with him and Terry Tolkin, who worked for Touch and Go at the time. We had just finished barbecuing, and I remember Terry saying to me, "You know, Dan, it's been about two years since your record has come out. Are you guys ready to do another one?" I think his idea was to do an EP. ●

Keith deep in concentration on stage at Teddy's in Milwaukee, c. 1985. Photo: Marty Graham.

A flyer for a Die Kreuzen gig at San Francisco's Mabuhay Gardens, c. 1986.

Growth, Transitions, and the Second Album

THE TOUR CYCLE FOR DIE KREUZEN'S DEBUT PROVED TO BE successful in establishing the band as an important part of the American hardcore underground, and the near-unanimous praise for the album only helped generate more interest in the band's live gigs. A situation like this would appear perfect from an outsider's perspective, but with great acclaim comes even greater expectations.

Few acts enjoy the level of critical acclaim that Die Kreuzen received after the release of their debut, but the band wasn't necessarily preparing themselves for it. How does one deal with relative success? While not absolute, there are essentially two options: build on the success achieved by continuing in a similar fashion or move in a new direction to keep things constantly evolving.

The band had no idea what would happen upon the release of the album. When they wrote and recorded the songs on the first album, above all else, they were just happy to be given the opportunity to make a full-length. It was never the band's intention to follow the Ramones blueprint of never straying from a single established sound. Even by comparison to *Cows and Beer*, the debut album sounds quite different. Undoubtedly one of the best in its genre, the first album in many ways ensured that the band had to evolve when the time came to record its follow-up.

With the band's writing and performances at an all-time high and equally strong production behind them, it's understandable why some could have viewed the first album and its relative success as the beginning of something—Die Kreuzen laying claim as one of hardcore's finest acts, preparing to follow it up with another record cut from the same cloth. In reality, though, it actually marked the end of that chapter for the band. Die Kreuzen's debut album didn't have multi-platinum sales to live up to, but the widespread acclaim it received inadvertently created artistic expectations for its follow-up. Sometimes, instead of trying to make a predictable next step, it's better to go somewhere else entirely.

Historically, plenty of artists have taken this path, refusing to follow up a massively successful album with a carbon copy of itself. Stevie Wonder's magnum opus, 1976's massively successful *Songs in the Key of Life*, remains one of pop music's best and most ambitious albums. Wonder himself could have continued down this path for at least another half-decade but instead chose to follow it up with an abstract, largely instrumental work, 1979's *Journey through the Secret Life of Plants*. Prince's enormously successful album and movie *Purple Rain* were followed up with his versions of a psychedelic pop daydream (1985's *Around the World in a Day*) and a hilarious black-and-white throwback (1986's *Under the Cherry Moon*). With the release of 1997's *OK Computer*, Radiohead had become one of the most critically acclaimed and beloved alternative-rock acts in the world, choosing to follow it up in 2000 with *Kid A*, an album that leaned heavily on electronics, samplers, and just about any other sound besides an electric guitar.

There were many acts of the more cookie-cutter variety who enjoyed varying levels of success during their brief windows of existence whose music sounded dated almost immediately. Die Kreuzen's boldness and indifference to following any rulebook not only made them stand apart from those acts, but it also helped futureproof their music. More than forty years later, Die Kreuzen's music still feels progressive, cutting-edge, and above all honest.

Making an artistic left turn is often seen as something to celebrate, the mark of an artist looking to challenge both themselves and their listeners. Regardless of whether their first album went completely unnoticed or sold millions, the band's broad musical tastes and need for self-satisfaction were always going to lead the way. Despite making one of the most celebrated hardcore punk records up to that point, the band's sonic expansion was a natural evolution; the music they were listening to was directly shaping the music they were creating. To repeat themselves would have been to consider only the wishes of their audience, and the band was going to move forward, whether their existing audience followed them or not.

Die Kreuzen began to find inspiration in a variety of other places. What made the self-titled album so special was nothing the band planned for; they simply went into the studio for a few days, tracked the songs, and called it a day. In writing, recording, and releasing the first album, Die Kreuzen achieved their exact vision at that time. It would be virtually impossible for them to try and recreate what they did on the debut, and attempting to do so would undermine everything that made that album special to begin with. Moving forward to the second album, they continued in the same fashion. This was the only guidance they needed.

Keith: By the time we put out that first record, I more or less had stopped listening to hardcore. I still loved those early records, but by that point I was really into what was coming out of England at that time. All of that English post-punk stuff. I loved Echo and the Bunnymen and Joy Division and Siouxie and the Banshees. That first REM record, too. I bought that when it came out and listened to it like twice a day every day.

Dan: We all loved Killing Joke and played them a lot at the time. I remember Erik turning me onto the Sisters of Mercy early on.

Erik: Dan said that I got him into Sisters of Mercy? Keith was the one who got me into them. I had this 1969 Pontiac Catalina and Keith and I went down to Chicago to see the Sisters of Mercy at the Exit. They were so good. They really knocked me out. One of the best things I've ever seen, easily.

Paul Mahern: For us in the Midwest, our connection to music was primarily through records. In the early days, you couldn't see a lot of those bands live. I think early on we were all much more influenced by record collections than being a part of a scene. I feel like you can definitely hear that in Die Kreuzen as well, especially in the later records.

Matt Sweeney: The Midwest thing that Die Kreuzen was coming out of, it was regional, but it was also inspired by these bigger rock bands who toured a lot. Midwest music has such a specific vibe, and then even more specific is Wisconsin, which is super-strange.

The need for music in the Midwest is just greater, the same way it is in England; at one point there were four *weekly* music magazines on one island. You know why? Because people took this shit seriously. It's grey outside, the weather sucks, nobody is telling you that you're cool, nobody is paying attention to your scene. In the Midwest, you must have a bigger imagination, go inward, get inspired, and do something with that. Die Kreuzen is such a prime example of that. They melted all these sounds and built this new thing with such great architecture and depth to it.

Erik: Previously, we would write a song and work really hard to play it as fast as we possibly could. After a while, it started feeling like a dead end. These were good songs, and we didn't want to be this one-trick pony where we were the fastest band in the land. It was great, it was fun, and I think we made a real statement with it, but that started to become difficult once we started to move on.

Keith: With the first album, we were working within the same sonic range for almost all the songs. With the second album, the songs were so different that approaching them in the same way as the last album just wouldn't have worked. That was part of it. Plus, after having done this for a while, we had more ideas of what we wanted to do. That first record was the first time any of us had ever been in a real recording studio before. Based on our experiences with that record and touring on it, we came into writing the second album with a lot more ideas and things we wanted to try out.

Brian: At that time, I was almost confused as to what was going on because I was so in love with hardcore. I knew there was some place to take it beyond what it had been, but I didn't know which way to take it, so I just played guitar as much as possible and listened to as much music as I possibly could. I was playing Metallica's *Ride the Lightning* a lot, for sure, but also stuff like Siouxsie and the Banshees and [the British post-punk band] the Flys—definitely a lot of the stuff that was coming out of England at the time.

Paul Mahern: I think that when you look at independent music at that time, you've got Hüsker Dü, the Effigies, Die Kreuzen, Articles of Faith, and they're all different from one another. Even on a national level, with Flipper and Black Flag and Dead Kennedys, all these bands had their own sound—there was no real set sound to being a punk rock band. I think early on in '81, '82, it felt like there was a lot more creativity. Everyone was taking the same energy but doing their own thing with it, because they were breaking new ground. Once you started getting closer to 1984, '85 was when hardcore developed a more specific sound. There was a uniformity you started to hear with a lot of the bands in the New York scene and a lot of those other second-generation bands; they all started to fall in line.

Thurston Moore: They came out of the gate fully formed with this super-fast hardcore thing, and I think for them it was just like . . . we could either write fifty more songs like this or we could move forward as a band. They had an interesting makeup because you could see that they were all into different stuff. You could tell that everyone in the band was kind of in their own zone, and together it was this pulling and pushing of styles. It wasn't across the board where everyone was on the same page as the Ramones. It was like, "Well, that guy over there is clearly into Joy Division and that guy over there is into Aerosmith and that guy over there is into Ornette Coleman."

The new songs weren't a complete left turn, of course. The band had a handful of newer songs in their repertoire when they recorded the first album but decided to let them develop more before committing them to tape. After more than a solid year of touring and practicing, they were ready to be tracked, along with a group of new ones.

Erik: When we were recording the first album, there was this feeling that we were marking an end of this part of what the band was doing ... if not an end, at the very least knowing that this was a statement of where we were at that point. By the time it came out, however many months later, we had new songs that we were writing that had a different feel.

Keith: People would ask us. "Are you gonna write more of that fast stuff?", and we'd just be like, "We did that already." The only reason why "Imagine a Light" and some of the faster songs ended up on that record was because we had them already, and it took us a really long time to finish songs. We never wrote songs that we didn't end up using. Those existed when we were recording the first album, but we decided to save them for the next album. Half of it is songs that we wrote around the time we were doing the first record, and the other half were newer things that we wrote over the course of the previous two years.

Thurston Moore: The idea was to grow with it, you know? To be a purist about it didn't make sense because it was just kind of something that you'd get out of your system. You had to grow up and the music had to grow with you, and if you didn't then you were just sort of being cookie-cutter with it. To me, Die Kreuzen were following that same path and doing it with a sort of legitimacy. I don't think they were trying to force the issue.

David Pajo: Hardcore was this wave that bands jumped on. Bad Brains and all of them created it and then people kinda rode the wave for a while. The idea as a hardcore band wasn't to sound exactly like the bands you idolized—the idea was to find your own sound. If you sounded exactly like another band, to me that was a turn-off. What was the point? I'd just rather listen to the band you're trying to sound like. To me, it was always about sounding like yourself. You could wear some influences on your sleeve, but if you sounded like someone else you were doing something wrong.

The first album's main concerns were quite sharply focused on speed, precision, and the unique tension that can only exist when combining the two. While some would try to take the music to an even faster and more frantic place, the band went in the opposite direction and started writing songs with slower tempos. In doing so, this allowed them to stretch out and explore odd time signatures and other things that were unconventional for a hardcore punk band. Their ability to stretch out and try new things in a practice setting was a direct result of them having the freedom and opportunity to do so. Much like the vats in San Francisco, rehearsal spaces in larger cities like Los Angeles and New York were hard to come by, with many of them often being available for rent on an hourly basis. Circumstances like these were not ideal for artists wanting to take their time and develop their sound. It's safe to say that Die Kreuzen's development and evolution as a band was at least partly a result of them being a Midwestern act. Had they lived elsewhere, it's debatable that they would have been able to grow in the manner that they did.

Brian: I used this technique for coming up with rhythms: I'd look at whatever was around me and try to rhythmically replicate what I saw. If it were two stones that were a certain distance apart from one another, I'd count it out a certain way and write based off that. I just kind of see music everywhere. Having a four-track recorder helped me realize what sounded good and what didn't. It helped me see if my ideas were any good or not.

Keith: Pretty much everything I came in with was in 3/4 time. At the beginning, time signatures didn't matter to us. People would tell us that all the time, like, "You can't do that," and we'd be like, "Why not?" Just leave that one note out and then start over to make it sound kinda cool. Erik and I were good at doing that, and we got good at going between 4/4 and 3/4 without any long transition.

By October of 1985, they had an entire album's worth of new songs ready to record. Returning to Multi-Track Studios again with Rick Canzano and Corey Rusk assisting with production, the band found themselves well-rehearsed and ready to commit their new ideas to tape. Unlike the sessions for their debut, however, the familiar environment led to a more comfortable and less rigid studio atmosphere.

Rick Canzano: The first thing I noticed was that the songs seemed like they were twice as long. They definitely had evolved and had become more thoughtful in their songwriting and musicality. Even though I had worked with them on their previous album and with other Touch and Go bands, the music was still very different from what I usually did. Because of that, I couldn't impart any color on their recordings; I wouldn't dare try to interfere with what they were doing.

Dan: I remember around this time that the control room was a little bit freer than it was the first time around. I remember recording my vocals and playing around with delays and reverbs. It was much more hands-on than the sessions for the first record. I think at one point Corey just left and let us do our thing.

Brian: A big part of my guitar sounds for this record was the Roland SD-1000 rack unit. It had a digital delay on it as well as some chorus effects. I would just set the chorus at 25% for the rate and 5% for the width to give it this really slow and rich sound.

Dan: We were really into green tea at the time, and I remember going into the other room to make myself a cup of tea, and I remember Keith busting into the room saying, "You gotta hear this!" Brian had just laid down an acoustic guitar track on "Man in the Trees," and they A/B'ed it, and you couldn't really tell that there was an acoustic guitar there, but when you played the song with and without the acoustic, it just sounded so much better.

Mike Gitter: That's where I think their color palate got a lot wider and a lot broader. In the context of the time that it was released, it wasn't that left-field. People forget what other bands were doing around that point. *October File* was very much a record as out of context as it is perceived. As brave as it seemed, it was also very much keeping in with other musicians from the punk scene.

Dan: We played one of the last rough mixes over the PA at this club called Greystone Hall in Detroit. I remember Corey not really knowing what to make of some of the songs, but he was definitely behind the album and behind our band.

Keith: There was never any indication that Corey wasn't going to put it out. At that point he was just putting out stuff by bands he liked, so whatever record it was that the band submitted, that was it, no questions asked. He always supported our growth as a band.

Corey Rusk: As a teenager in the late '70s, new wave and punk were being birthed simultaneously and there were great bands that wore both monikers. It was all so creative and interesting and different from anything else that was available before, and I liked so much of it. Everything from the early Pere Ubu and Devo records to Suicide to the early Joy Division and Cure records, I loved all that as well as all the hardcore bands at the time, so I started hearing some of the newer songs—it was just like, "Wow, this is awesome."

Brian: I love what we did and I'm proud of it. The song I love Dan's vocals on the most is "Imagine a Light." The way he plays off of the melodies, where his voice comes in and creates this atonal explosion, it's just amazing.

The album was definitely a stylistic progression for the band, marking the beginning of their exploration with melody yet still maintaining the darkness and dissonance of their early output. Visually too, the album looked different from anything hardcore had seen up to that point, thanks to the artistic prowess of Richard Kohl.

Sonically, the music that shaped the album came from places outside of just the world of punk and hardcore. Acts like the Birthday Party, Dead Can Dance, and Bauhaus were all on 4AD Records, the U.K.-based indie label known for its distinct visual aesthetic and enigmatic presence. Much like the music on *October File*, the album art was also a nod to early output of 4AD.

Richard Kohl: This was really the only time I was ever given any kind of directive from the band. I had done ink drawings for *Cows and Beer* and for the first record, so all they said to me was to do something different. They wanted each record to have its own kind of identity, which I thought was a really good idea. From this record on, I'd ask them just two things—give me a title for the record and a tape of the music. They'd give me these really ambiguous titles that you could really make mean anything. I'd never literally translate them visually; in fact, I almost always wanted to do the opposite of that.

I was really into all the 4AD bands. The packaging was always really gorgeous. Records are this really cool medium that should be packaged well and they should be special.

They sent me the tape of *October File* and it really blew me away. It was a logical progression; they definitely were getting much better. They were thinking outside of the box. I loved what they were doing rhythmically, getting really angular with the rhythms. Erik Tunison? Good lord, what a great drummer. The fact that he is such a great drummer as well as a fantastic human being . . . boy, there must be a God.

I kinda used that as a springboard to see what would pop into my head. Lots of times, that's exactly how it happened. The only thing I can think of that influenced that would be like . . . shadow puppetry. That album cover was very fun, simple, and happened very quickly. I had an easel that I had flat and taped a big sheet of rice paper from the sidebars of it. I had all this stupid useless junk just lying around, and I put pieces of that behind the rice paper and then I backlit it. You could play with it and make the shadows do really bizarre things.

The next step was photographing it, but I didn't have a camera. At the time, I was working as a delivery person at this big commercial photo lab, and everyone there had access to cameras. I had the guy who was my dispatcher come over and take the photos and he immediately told me, "No, this is not going to work at all," and I told him to shut up and just start shooting stuff with different exposure settings and stuff and just see what happens. That was over the weekend, and Monday I showed up at work really early, and he already cranked out a proof sheet of the photos. He was so excited, I remember him saying, "This stuff looks so fuckin' cool, I would've never believed that we could make this work." He was just thrilled.

I blew the image up and cropped it a bit. This time around with the text, I wanted it to be a little bit cleaner than I did on the first record. They

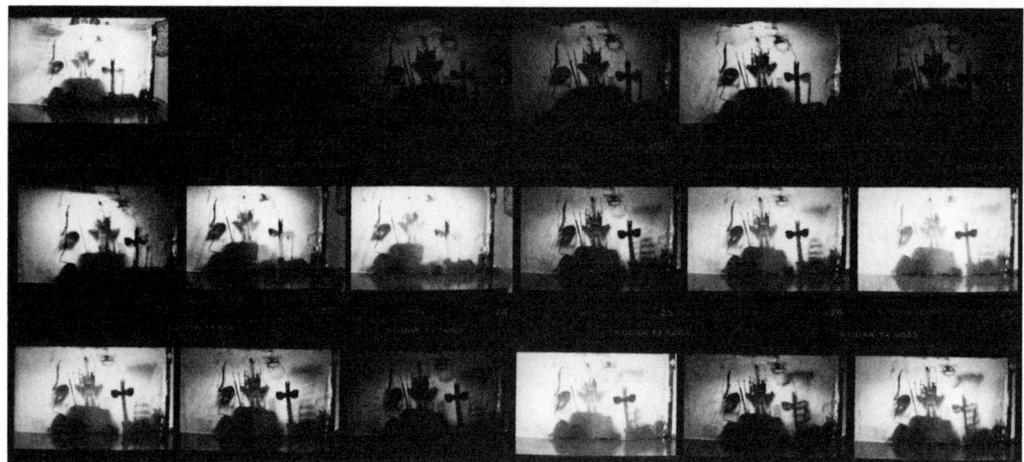

Above: Detail of Richard Kohl's original contact sheet for the *October File* album cover featured the shadows of random objects against a backlight sheet of paper. Photo courtesy of Richard Kohl.

Below: The completed cover.

embossed the lettering on it too, which was nice. It kind of elevated it to another level.

Kim Thayil: I loved the *October File* album cover. It felt like a progression for Richard as well, where the first record cover was more drawing-based, this one was more photography and maybe mixed media? It was different, but it still felt like it was done by the same guy. That guy is so amazing. Even though he changed things visually, aesthetically it still felt the same. You could tell that it was him doing it. That whole "don't judge a book by its cover" thing? With *October File*, I absolutely could! The way that record looked was *exactly* how it sounded.

Still, *October File* was only the beginning of the band's journey away from hardcore. It marked the start of a pattern that we would see for the remainder of the band's career: on each album, one can hear echoes of both its predecessor and successor. Building on the ambiance and atmosphere of the debut, *October File* introduced new sounds and textures into the band's sonic palette, most notably a slower and more melodic approach to songwriting.

Beginning with the distant and echoey whispers of Egeness's guitar, *October File*'s opener, "Man in the Trees," serves as an apt introduction to the album. Kubinski's signature screams were there, as was Brammer and Tunison's locked-in rhythm section, but both were presented side by side with a more pronounced melodic sensibility. It's a very strong album opener, perhaps the band's strongest, in that it very beautifully bridges the old with the new.

"Uncontrolled Passion" and "Imagine a Light" date back to the debut album and not surprisingly are the most familiar-sounding tracks on the album. "Uncontrolled Passion" is slightly reminiscent of "In School" with its winding bass and guitar riffs, while "Imagine a Light" is the album's most straight-ahead-hardcore moment. It has all the elements that made their debut so memorable, delivered at maximum speed. "Imagine a Light" benefits from being an outlier, and presenting it side by side with slower and more melodic material makes it sound especially intense.

October File showcases the band's growth in a variety of ways, one of them being the incorporation of odd time signatures into their sound. "Hear and Feel" is the earliest example of this on the album, with its driving 3/4-time groove. It's more midtempo than most of the songs on the self-titled first album, but its running time makes it no less efficient, getting in and out in ninety seconds. Two tracks later, "Conditioned" takes the twisted terror of their debut and sets it in 5/4 time. The odd time gives it a menacing quality that it wouldn't have otherwise and allows the band to build on their sound that's already quite developed as is. Neither of these forays into more technical songwriting feels out of reach, though, and the band incorporates these new elements into their sound in a very comfortable way.

The dirges of "Cool Breeze" and "There's a Place" take the darker elements and atmospheres of their first album to new places, marking the first instances of noticeably slower songwriting for the band. In the same way that the debut album's focus on speed showcased the band's gift for precision, these two tracks are an exercise in patience and understanding, specifically the latter. The acoustic guitars and overt melodicism of "Cool Breeze" immediately stand out, though they still fit into the sound and aesthetic of both the album and band overall. "There's a Place" feels like a sibling of "All White," and, while it may not share an eventual uptick in tempo, it maintains a twisted and ominous Black Sabbath-esque mood that sits well next to *My War*-era Black Flag, Flipper, and Swans.

One major difference between *October File* and the self-titled first album was a conscious decision not to include the song lyrics. Kubinski has always kept his lyrics close to the chest, preferring that the listeners assign whatever meaning they wish to the songs. This may or may not be related to his change in vocal style for the album. A more melodic approach is obvious upon first listen, but the slower tempos allow Kubinski to stretch out a bit vocally and, because of this, we hear Kubinski trading in the rapid-fire delivery of the first album for something a bit more mysterious and enigmatic. It allows the vocals to become more of an additional instrument as opposed to just the sound of the person delivering them.

While there are a handful of exceptions, much of *October File* would sound very close to the songs on the first album if they were played considerably faster. The chord progressions, riffs, and rhythms are all quite similar to the material on the band's debut, just played at a much slower pace, which makes them feel more dissimilar than they actually are. Live footage of them in 1985 features plenty of *October File* songs alongside older material, and hearing them played slightly faster, coming through a blown-out PA system in a basement, their resemblance to the first album is much easier to hear.

If the debut album was the sound of a band establishing itself among the best of American hardcore punk, *October File* was them showing that they had ambitions far beyond the parameters they had set for themselves with the debut. Prior to Die Kreuzen, few acts in the punk scene strayed away from their roots; many broke up before even getting the opportunity to do so.

The Clash's triple album *Sandinista!* is one of the earliest examples of a punk rock band breaking from the limitations of the genre. The Clash themselves had already flirted with the likes of reggae, jazz, and R&B on their previous album, *London Calling*, but *Sandinista!* went even further, with the band exploring the likes of dub, gospel, and calypso. While critically successful, the album has always been a point of contention among its fan base, with some citing the album as a brilliant work of artful eclecticism and others completely dismissing it as just another example of overblown excess. Its merits remain divisive among music fans to this day.

Sandinista! aside, anyone expecting Die Kreuzen to repeat the first album would be asking them to compromise their integrity. As the band began to branch out beyond the rigid "loud and fast" rules of hardcore, so many of their direct influences were doing the same. John Lydon all but abandoned the conventional rock and roll of the Sex Pistols with Public Image Ltd. The Damned were well into their goth phase. Wire began to focus on the spaces between the notes.

The band's contemporaries were beginning to branch out as well. Hüsker Dü continued their exploration with melody on *New Day Rising*. Black Flag got glacial with *My War*. Even Void, the short-lived Washington, D.C., band known for their endearingly unstable brand of hardcore, recorded *Potion for Bad Dreams*, an album so far from their initial work that it remains unreleased to this day.

While certain press outlets understood and praised *October File*, others weren't quite so sure what to make of it. For all its celebration and reverence, the first album's near-unanimous acclaim also meant that someone would inadvertently be let down by its follow-up solely because it wasn't the first album.

Just two years after the brightest of endorsements for the band's debut album, *Maximum Rocknroll* felt quite different about its follow-up. "This is a fucking boring record. This is a fucking bor . . . nah . . . pretty unmemorable stuff," wrote Tim Yohannan in July of 1986. "The speed is down, but so is

the spark, leaving those still-ragged vocals and an R.E.M. meets LED ZEP sound. Wish I could be excited, but I'm not."

When looking at punk's first wave, many of the bands had at the very least an appreciation for music outside of the confines of the genre. By comparison, hardcore audiences were often less open to new sounds, and as a result bands who chose to branch out often found a less than ideal reception to their new material. If the fans were to dictate the music, there's a good chance that the genre would have stopped evolving after *GI*.

Though less obvious to hear, one needs to remember that Die Kreuzen were music fans first and foremost and that their playing styles were informed by Bowie and Rush as much as by Black Flag and the Germs. The first album, with all of its speed and precision, sounded the way it did because of those other influences; *October File* merely took that album's spaciousness and atmosphere and used it as the new foundation for songwriting.

Corey Rusk: In a way, I can see both sides of it. If you make one of the best hardcore albums ever, the people whose favorite form of music is just that, they're going to want your next record to be that, and even more so.

Ian MacKaye: A band like Sonic Youth evolved, they kept playing but people were along for the journey. The difference with them is that they didn't come from something like hardcore, which was such a revolutionary musical form at that time. It was almost impossible to shake it off.

Matt Sweeney: When an artist or band is fucking excellent, when they really just ring the bell with a specific thing, people get so pissed if they don't keep ringing that bell. It's kind of a strange comparison, but Cat Stevens went through that. He was this fucking huge pop star, and then he went prog. People just couldn't get on board with it, and then he stopped making music altogether. People, particularly Americans, were just like, "Oh, fuck that dude, he's not giving me what I want." With Die Kreuzen, no one was making hardcore as tight and ferocious as them, so when they stopped doing it people started to resent them—like, "Who the fuck do you think you are?"

The whole hardcore thing and the way it's looked at can be so insanely conservative. What better band to prove the point than Die Kreuzen? They mastered it—they played faster and more passionately than anybody did—so of course they had to take it somewhere else.

Kim Thayil: There were so many people who were so preoccupied with showing everyone how punk they were—they acted a certain way, dressed a certain way, and had certain opinions. They show allegiance to something that they believe is true, their ideal of the cultural tenants of punk rock. If that's what it is, then punk rock sucks. Those people can stay stuck where they are and have their identity. Go be king of the block, buddy.

Neko Case: Hardcore might be the most fascist fucking music that I was also deeply into at one point [laughs]. People are really nostalgic about it now, but for me it feels a bit dogmatic at times.

Jon Wurster: That odd hardcore rulebook that somehow came to be, that most people followed? That's why everyone jumped off at some point, because it became so boring and so unremarkable. That's what was so great about Die Kreuzen—they didn't stick to the rulebook; they burned the rulebook.

Steve Albini: To the extent that they were a hardcore band, that was the least significant thing about their identity. They were disaffected kids from Milwaukee, first. They were as much a product of the skate park as much as they were the hardcore scene. I didn't feel like there was a betrayal or a loss when they decided that they were going to get more expansive.

October File is still a very interesting document in that it's such a stark contrast to the first record. They were trying to solve the riddle of playing in a more sophisticated style without having a roadmap, without having a specific method that they could follow. They were trying to become more sophisticated or more involved musically, and they were trying to figure it out on their own. Most of it seems just like genuine invention on their part again.

Paul Mahern: I never thought that they lost that post-punk edge that I heard in them from the beginning. It made sense to me. When I saw them for the first time, that was all there. The first record was definitely them at their most aggressive, but when *October File* came out, to me that was like a return to what they were doing a little earlier than that.

Lou Barlow: They got even cooler once they moved onto *October File*. They went from hardcore into something more interesting, instead of metal, which a lot of bands did. Around 1984, '85, when a lot of that homespun speed-metal stuff started happening and a lot of people started moving in that direction, it just wasn't all that interesting to me. When Die Kreuzen moved on, they got weirder and gothier, which was so much cooler to me.

Bob Nastanovich: With *October File,* it was just a classic maturation. Like, how long can you continue playing that fast, you know? They got a little more weird and dark. You can feel the transition happening in real time, and you can get bits and pieces of why that band was great at doing both things.

Nathan Larson (member, Swiz, Shudder to Think): *October File* sounded like a big smashed-up version of everything that was happening at the moment. It had elements of hardcore but also things like early REM, and that was combined with this really cool and different kind of vocal approach. It wasn't screaming, but it wasn't fully melodic, it was so hard to tell what he [Dan] was up to, but it sounded fantastic. There was this really uneasy and unsettling quality to what they were doing, but not in a bad way. It's hard to articulate, but there's something really spooky and literary about it. Hearing a song like "Man in the Trees" with the way it starts, it's just, like, so creepy, it gives me goosebumps.

Brad Wood: Die Kreuzen were always more inscrutable and more difficult to really know. They didn't hold back on the atonality, they never catered to the audience—they were just unknowable. *October File* is such a dense, dark, and disquieting record.

Neko Case: My dear friend Trevor Lanigan, who is no longer with us—I think he gave me a tape of *October File.* I was totally obsessed, and I never looked back from there. They were so melodic, and that was what made me deeply love them so much. As they grew and started to slow things down, especially on *October File,* they were just stretching out and creating space for melody. I loved them as a hardcore band but something about *October File* was this brand-new thing. It was a different world. There's something about the guitar tone on *October File* that doesn't sound like anything else, with that Kramer aluminum-neck guitar. I actually bought one of those guitars because of *October File.*

Mike Gitter: In a lot of ways, if we look at modern culture, a lot of the musical ambitions of people just doing it because they don't know any better, that forged the sound of underground indie music and modern mainstream music. Die Kreuzen are very much a part of that.

Dennis Lyxzen: My mind was wide open, and I didn't really think about it as them being a hardcore band. At that time, I was so into Touch and Go as a label, so when I heard *October File,* to me it just fit in with a lot of what Touch and Go had put out. It wasn't in the mindset of a hardcore band, I didn't really connect the lineage of it at the time. It's in a similar vein as Black Flag with *My War.* As crazy and chaotic as that first Die Kreuzen record was, as the band progressed, they kept that element in their sound, but it just showed itself in different ways.

It would have been so easy for them to repeat themselves because they had success with that first record, and they could have easily just kept doing that same thing. But if you're into music and an artist, you always want to develop. They feel like a band that never played it safe, and that's pretty amazing.

Jon Wurster: I remember having a copy of *Spin* where they reviewed *October File,* and it had this great photo of them in there. I remember thinking just once again about how great they looked and how I couldn't wait to buy the record. I bought the record in the mall of the town that I grew up in. I was amazed that this suburban mall had a copy of it.

I just remember really liking that record and what they were doing because it was so different from what most of these bands that started in hardcore were doing. There was a lot of art-rock kind of stuff happening on that record, but they also started to experiment with melody, especially with "Man in The Trees."

Kim Thayil: All the things I loved about the first album were the things that made them stand out, so when I heard *October File* I thought, "Aha!" because it totally made sense. It was obvious to me that these guys had this album in them—it was just brilliant. The song titles, too, just looked like they were written by someone who was literate and not just inspired by whatever rock band he saw last weekend—way more inspired by books and movies. Band names help, song titles and album titles help, album art helps. You look at that album cover, and it makes you stop and realize that these guys come from a community associated with really great visual artists and photographers. It gives you context as to what the band is about.

At the time, I kinda thought that Die Kreuzen was doing something that Green River would have done if they were able to. I think it had to do with the vocals, because vocally Dan sounded similar to Mark Arm. Still, that probably wasn't fair of me, because Die Kreuzen was so much more progressive. Green River's thing was some weird hybrid of, like, the Dead

Boys and New York Dolls with more glam kinda stuff. Die Kreuzen was doing weird time-signature stuff and had weird chord progressions. It wasn't until years later that I realized, "Wait, what was I thinking? This is way more like what Soundgarden was doing."

For all the people who didn't understand the album and the band's progression, plenty of others did. *The Village Voice*'s Chuck Eddy praised the album's precision and diverse influences, calling it "art rock from hell." *Forced Exposure*'s John Komp wrote, "It's so good to see a band as virtuosic as Die Kreuzen snap the bindings that might have held them immobile until withered, like so many others . . . it is obvious, even definite, that this sound will please many more, and disappoint very few."

Comparing the band to Aerosmith, Wire, the Birthday Party, and Einstürzende Neubauten among many others, Steve Albini wrote a review of the album in the fanzine *Matter* that's about as far from the *Maximum Rocknroll* review as one can get: "Forget for a moment all the things associated with the phrase. Try for just a second to hear the words as they were spoken in this context for the first time. Hard Core. Yeah. Severe, powerful, unrelenting rock noise, with the beat hyped up and the songs overloaded with unrestrained enthusiasm, savvy and sheer grunt. Forget that an idiom has developed which parrots those sentiments without delivering on any of them. Imagine a band that could not just fulfill but reinvent at every turn. Oh, you mean Die Kreuzen? Yeah."

The less aggressive tilt of some of the songs on *October File* resulted in people outside of the hardcore punk underground hearing the record, most notably A&R people at major labels. In 1986, the idea of an independent band signing to a major label was relatively, though not completely, new. Hüsker Dü and the Replacements had both signed with Warner Brothers–related labels. It was only a matter of time before the band themselves started to attract the attention of majors.

Early on, the band was approached by Profile Records, the label best known for releases by Run-DMC. Like many deals given to young independent bands at the time, though, it was far from an ideal arrangement.

Keith: Profile Records called Corey, who passed their contact info onto us. He was just kinda, "Do whatever what you want, I don't know if I recommend this but maybe see what they have to say." We got in touch with them and got a contract from them which we took to our friend Paul New's brother-in-law or something who was a lawyer.

Brian: They must've thought we were some yokels from Wisconsin who would take the first offer they got. I think they assumed that we wouldn't take it to a lawyer. We took it to Robert Leidenbaum. He just laughed.

Keith: He was just like, "Wow, I can't believe they would send you this if they knew that you were going to have a lawyer look it over." It was just completely all in their favor—"We'll give you guys .5 cents per album sold and we have the right to do whatever we want with the album" and all this kind of stuff.

Brian: Basically, they'd take our first born [laughs]. Complete control over everything. If we decided to leave the label, we couldn't be a band because they'd own the Die Kreuzen name.

Dan: It allowed them complete artistic and creative freedom with us, pretty much. They could do whatever they wanted with the album art, they could remix tracks, all kinds of stuff. It was just one thing after another with those guys.

Richard Kohl: It seemed really insane. They talked about that at great lengths when they were interviewed for *Forced Exposure*. I had talked to them before the interview came out, and it really just sounded shady as hell. Why would Profile Records want a punk band? It just seemed like such a ripoff.

While the offer from Profile proved to be a bust, this wouldn't be the last time that a major label showed interest in the band. The new melodic direction the band started to take with *October File* allowed their music to be heard outside of their default audience, and it was around this time that people started to see Die Kreuzen's potential outside of it. It began with a review in *College Music Journal*, usually shortened by readers as *CMJ*.

For the punk and hardcore world, reviews circulated largely through a network of fanzines. The gap between punk and what was on top-forty radio was filled by what was referred to as "college rock," a term that applied to everyone from REM and the Replacements to Hüsker Dü. *CMJ* did for the world of college rock what fanzines like *Maximum Rocknroll* and *Flipside* did for punk and hardcore.

Brian Egeness with the quintessential smoking guitarist pose at the Newport Music Hall in Columbus, Ohio, in 1986. Photo: Jay Brown.

In a short review of *October File* in their June 1986 issue, they wrote, "Die Kreuzen is not hardcore, not metal, not doomy British new wave or American pop music; they are all these things and they are none of them. They are destined for great things—someday they may be as big as Metallica"—a flattering prediction to make, certainly.

In the same way that the glowing *Maximum Rocknroll* review of the first album convinced many to check out the album, *CMJ*'s review of *October File* served as an entry point for many readers, among them Michael Alago, the Elektra A&R executive responsible for signing Metallica to the label.

Michael Alago (A&R, Elektra Records): I have always been a curious person both professionally and personally. As an A&R executive at Elektra, I would scour the USA and get all the music 'zines, newspapers, magazines, and flyers left at clubs from my favorite cities and check out the music section for live gigs and record reviews. Then I'd just trust my instincts if something sounded good.

I saw Die Kreuzen being reviewed in *CMJ*, and I liked what I read. By then, I had signed Metallica, and every reviewer thought a comparison was necessary, but I ignored that part of the review. I got in touch with the label.

Paul Mahern: I'll say for the record right now—Metallica were never even a patch on the coat of Die Kreuzen.

Matt Sweeney: I went to a Catholic boys' school, and a lot of kids were from Union, which was like *the* metal stronghold in New Jersey. That whole Metallica and Slayer wave was huge where I was from. I remember being a pretentious little skateboarder dick, and at the time I remember telling people, "Die Kreuzen fucking kills all that stuff." I really chose to take a side and was always putting Die Kreuzen in the face of Metallica fans.

Of course, a month later I realized that it was all good, but I really remember wondering how people couldn't understand that Die Kreuzen was the heaviest, coolest, most forward-thinking and mysterious band on the planet.

Corey Rusk: By then, the majors were sniffing around indie labels, so I wasn't shocked when Michael contacted us. To me it made sense that anyone would be interested because they were a great band.

As a label, you hope that your bands don't leave and go someplace else, especially because you're not doing it to get rich. It would have been heartbreaking if they left at that point and signed to a major, but at the same time we were working with bands on an album-to-album basis. It's not like they owed us three albums or anything. All of the bands I worked with I considered to be friends, so it wasn't like I was going to hide Michael's contact information from them. Basically, at the end of the day, I wasn't going to be a dick and not pass it along. Whatever came of that would just be what it was.

Michael Alago: I got in touch with Erik, gave him a phone call, introduced myself, and asked for the LP. I got it and was blown away by the intense energy and atmosphere of the tunes.

Dan: We played a set at the Foolkiller in Kansas City. We came out and just played *October File* straight through while the audience sat in chairs and just kind of watched us, not really knowing what to make of it. I think we eventually got some applause, but people were more confused by it than anything else.

Keith: I can't blame people. It was brand-new and probably hard to process. Hüsker Dü used to do that all the time, though. They'd come through town and play their entire new album that hadn't been released yet and then maybe a handful of old songs for an encore. People would get really mad, but I loved it. I remember playing with them in Chicago and they came out and played all of *Zen Arcade* and just being completely blown away. It was more about showing our audience exactly where we were at that point in time.

Jon Wurster: Back then at the University of Pennsylvania there was this kind of hip punk rock frat that would put on shows. There was a show that Die Kreuzen and the Offenders played. I had a friend that went to the show, and I asked him how it was, and I remember him saying something like, "Die Kreuzen were great. They were this hardcore band, but they had these pop songs." They must have already started playing some of the stuff off of the next record.

Greg Anderson: I saw Die Kreuzen in 1986 in Tacoma at the Crescent Ballroom. They always had, like, five to seven bands on the bill. The fact that they came to Seattle at all definitely meant something to the people there. Not a lot of people played Seattle back then because it was so tucked away. All-ages shows had dried up there, so a lot of bands would skip it and go play Portland instead. A lot of bands who even bothered to come

Above: Die Kreuzen tag their name on the wall of a club. Photo courtesy of Die Kreuzen.

Below: Die Kreuzen play Chicago's Cabaret Metro in support of *October File,* 1986. Photo courtesy of Die Kreuzen.

up to Seattle at all ended up doing well here and leaving a lasting impact on the music scene. It was a really receptive audience. People just wanted to hear music because they were kind of starved for it in a way.

Neko Case: I saw them at the Crescent Ballroom in Tacoma, and they were second to last on the bill. I was just so excited to see them because I had been a fan for a little while. They were so fucking good, and I was not at all disappointed.

A lot of those shows at the time were super male-dominated with these, like, part-time military dudes with mohawks who loved doing meth. There'd be, like, a thousand of those at the shows and they'd always just be saying the worst shit about women. Those kinda dudes were definitely around, and some of them were in bands. It really was that level of, like, crazy caveman. Die Kreuzen were different in that they never gave me even a hair of doubt about them. They never felt like this overly masculine thing.

Matt Sweeney: There's a feminine quality to them, but it's married to this weird phantasmagorical scariness, like a real sense of that gray black Midwestern loneliness.

David Pajo: There was this sort of machismo punk scene, but Touch and Go always felt separate from that. Touch and Go had this very smart quality to the label and the bands they worked with. Even Killdozer, who totally sounded like they'd be these sorta macho guys, were totally the opposite. Really literate, academic type guys.

Matt Sweeney: I remember I saw a photo of them [Die Kreuzen] and thought, "Who the fuck are these guys?" because they looked *amazing*. Particularly with *October File*, that photo of them standing there with the tall grass and weeds, they just looked so fuckin' cool. Dan Kubinski's footwear was on point. Every single dude looked cool and had their own look. They just looked like a band. Brian was like the mad scientist guy, Erik looked like this cool metal dude, Keith was like the coolest looking goth guy, and then Kubinski looked like a cool stoner. Just the presentation in that single photo was just so perfect—it was so cool and disturbing. I'm from New Jersey and I grew up really close to the city, but there's this sense of the suburban with Die Kreuzen, but also with this kind of smoky, shitty city background. It was just so powerful. ●

Century Days

THOUGH THE AMERICAN AND EUROPEAN UNDERGROUND scenes were thriving both critically and artistically, record sales were modest in comparison to the million-sellers that appeared hourly on MTV. Bands were releasing some of the best albums of their careers, but critical acclaim can only sell so many records, and many found themselves feeling displaced: too underground for the mainstream and too mainstream for the underground.

That isn't to say that there weren't success stories. Development deals were common at this time, and labels put resources, money, and, above all, patience into the bands, with hopes that the acts would finally start to generate results. While this model didn't always prove to be successful, it worked for a handful of acts that went on to release some of the era's defining music. REM and the B52s were both prime examples of American underground bands who toiled nonstop, allowing their fanbases to grow gradually. By the end of the '80s, both acts enjoyed sizable mainstream breakthroughs, largely due to the work that preceded them.

Yet in the American underground, subgenres were once again mutating into new and different styles. Hardcore punk's biggest acts had split. The Germs, Dead Kennedys, Black Flag, Minor Threat were all things of the past. An entirely new crop of bands from the East Coast picked up the torch and carried it for the remaining decade, inspiring and influencing others the way that the aforementioned acts had inspired them. Kids who came to the bands just a little too late were filtering them through other influences, and what came out was an honest expression of their reality. New acts from cities like Boston and New York took the sound of the first-wave acts and combined them with a notable Bay Area thrash influence and a more outwardly masculine presentation. The tempos mostly remained fast and, though the music didn't always bear a similar resemblance to the genre's originators, music needs to progress.

Other acts in the underground took the sound of early-'80s East Coast and Midwestern hardcore to different places entirely. Sonic Youth borrowed from the genre's more experimental nature, Big Black took its distortion to new levels of terror, and Dinosaur Jr fell somewhere in the middle, marrying both of those elements with a heavy Neil Young influence. Hüsker Dü, who were directly associated with hardcore early on, continued their evolution away from it, moving toward more traditional melody-driven songwriting. Similarly, cities like Washington, D.C., which contributed greatly to the genre's first wave, continued to look to the future, with new acts like Rites of Spring, Grey Matter, Shudder to Think, and Fugazi laying the foundation for post-hardcore.

Die Kreuzen were part of this continually evolving musical landscape. The band never made conscious efforts to reinvent themselves, but their progressive and wide-reaching tastes ensured that their writing was constantly shaped by new sounds. There was also a desire to continue to outdo themselves with each subsequent release. The band spent the previous two albums working with Rick Canzano in Michigan and wanted to work with someone new for the follow-up to *October File*. While Canzano did his best, given his minimal understanding of and exposure to the genre, his frame of reference for a band like Die Kreuzen was limited. For their third album, they chose to work with a local Wisconsin engineer who was beginning to make a name for himself in pockets of the underground. Based in Madison, he owned and operated Smart Studios, and cut his teeth recording many local punk and hardcore bands. His name was Butch Vig.

Vig's previous recordings of Mecht Mensch and the Tar Babies meant that he had a great frame of reference for music of an aggressive nature. Additionally, his recent work with acts like Killdozer showed that he was well versed in the more progressive sounds of the post-hardcore era. His approach was a wonderfully delicate balance between lo-fi grit and hi-fidelity sheen, and it resulted in some of the best sounding independent releases of the era.

Vig and Steve Marker founded Smart Studios in 1983 in Madison, Wisconsin's capital city roughly ninety minutes west of Milwaukee. Immediately upon opening their doors, Smart's goal was to provide affordable recordings for anyone who needed them, with their client list including friends and contemporaries of Die Kreuzen like Mecht Mensch, the Appliances-SFB, and the Tar Babies. Smart quickly rose in the ranks as one of the region's go-to facilities for independent bands seeking affordable but high-quality recordings. The recordings coming out of Smart struck that careful balance between too much and not enough, presenting bands with a recording that was hi-fi while still retaining a grit. Acts could sound absolutely massive without losing their edge, and over time people began to take notice of Vig's work, specifically his work with Madison sludge kings Killdozer.

Corey Rusk: The whole world needs to know that Butch Vig's path to becoming Butch Vig started with Killdozer. Killdozer was recording with him from the very beginning, before anyone knew or cared who they were. People would just ask about where the Killdozer records were recorded. It's because of those Killdozer records that Die Kreuzen, as well as other bands like Laughing Hyenas and Urge Overkill, came to know of Butch.

Dan: Butch Vig's recordings sounded so crisp and full. I heard them and thought, "Man, we need to do a record with him."

Keith: Butch had worked with Killdozer and Laughing Hyenas and we thought those records sounded great. Those Hyenas records especially are still just the most fucking awesome-sounding records ever.

Butch Vig (owner, Smart Studios, producer, *Century Days*): Bands from Madison who were familiar with the Milwaukee scene would talk about Die Kreuzen a lot. Corey Rusk had been talking them up to me quite a bit as well, but I wasn't really all that familiar with those first two records.

I remember seeing them perform at the WAMI [Wisconsin Area Music Industry] Awards, and my initial impression was that they were fucking amazing. They stood out from all the other acts there because of how unique their sound was. They were so many different things—it was psychedelic rock, it was punk, it was almost metal at points, and yet they had this great pop sensibility to their songs as well. I thought they were pretty amazing, and they looked so fucking cool. They kind of blew everyone away at the WAMIs; I can't even remember anyone else who performed that night.

I think Erik sent me a cassette of them rehearsing some of the new songs, and right off the bat I could hear that it was quite different. I knew that making the record was going to be interesting and fun.

Keith: It was always based on assembling parts together. We'd chart things out on a dry-erase board when we were writing. The one thing we were adamant about was not repeating ourselves. If we ever wrote something that sounded like something that we had already done, we'd throw it out immediately. We were much more interested in moving forward than repeating ourselves. That's why it took so long for us between records: we really took our time to write songs that didn't sound like things we had already done before.

Butch Vig: I never really made a conscious decision to compare what I was doing to the old stuff. I was personally excited that the new material was much more interesting and less one-dimensional. They had all these different styles that they were starting to incorporate into the music, and I was really excited to work on them.

Milwaukee and Madison are separated by seventy miles of uneventful interstate driving. Everyone wanted to make the most of the limited time and budget they had, so they decided to meet halfway in Waukesha, Wisconsin, tracking at Breezeway Studios during the evenings.

Butch Vig: Breezeway had a nice Neotek console and some nice microphones, but it was a pretty barebones studio. The tracking room was nice, but it sounded kind of dead. I really wanted the record to have more of a live sound and feel to it, so I had to use some compressors and reverbs to bring it to life a little more. On the first day of tracking, the owner of the place just said, "Here's the keys," and left. We never saw him for the rest of the session. It was just the band and me. The guy gave us a dirt-cheap rate to come in after hours. We knew going in that we could stretch the budget a little more. We worked on and off over the course of about a month.

Keith: It was cheaper to do it during the off hours, so we'd start at like 9 p.m. and go until, like, 4 a.m. I remember we'd be coming back really late at night, and I had to go into work at Atomic Records the next day; [I was] just totally out of it.

Dan: We'd do, like, two or three days at a time and then come back later for a few more days. I think the whole album ended up taking close to about two weeks to make. We got a really good deal on the studio by coming in after hours and then tracking into the early morning. But then we'd have to be at our day jobs the next day, so it was rough.

Keith: We went in, and I think we did bass and drums together, and then Brian played along with us. Erik and I would just blast out the basic tracks. Getting sounds always takes a little bit, but once it got down to recording, I think we got most of the things in two or three takes at the most. The songs were all finished being written before we entered the studio, so there really wasn't much experimentation in terms of arrangements or specific parts. I think, for us, the experimentation came with the overall sound of the album.

Brian: Butch was open to ideas. He jumped head-on into the creative side of it and allowed us to experiment. I started becoming interested in engineering, and Butch let me get behind the board at those sessions, which was great.

He was definitely a producer. I remember him walking around the room and hitting the snare drum, trying to find the sweet spot in the room. Once he found it, that's where he set Erik's drums up, and the drums sounded incredible.

Dan: We always wanted to make the best record we possibly could; that was always the goal. Even though working with Butch resulted in us making records that sounded better, that was always our goal from the beginning.

Butch Vig: We didn't have time to rehearse the songs or work on arrangements beforehand, so I would suggest things on the fly as they were being tracked, but for the most part those songs were done when we started tracking. We didn't have a ton of time to make the record, but I was lucky that they had played together a lot and were ready to go once it started. We never really had to do more than a handful of takes to cut a basic track. I wanted to get the sound of the band playing in the room to come across on the recording.

They had a few things working in their favor that gave them that distinctive sound. One was how each individual member approached their role in the band. Erik's style of drumming is very unique. It's very tribal and propulsive; he wasn't playing those basic Ringo-style kick-and-snare backbeats. Brian's guitar playing could be psychedelic, metal, folky and at times, just noisy and bizarre. Keith was always laying down these monster bass grooves, but he also wrote these really hooky basslines. Dan had this amazing range with what he could do with his voice. He could sing melodically, but he could also do that awesome scream that he was known for, and he'd sometimes do both within the course of the same line.

As a band, they had this incredible sense of dynamics. They all had different perspectives, but it was really the four of them and their unique individual identities that made up the sound of Die Kreuzen. Some bands have a singular sensibility that all the members are tuned in to, but, to me, the four of them all had different sensibilities and approaches, and I think more than anything else that was what made up the sound of Die Kreuzen.

Keith: We were always listening to new music. Working in record stores gives you that advantage. It wasn't so much that it influenced our songwriting because we were really adamant about not repeating ourselves or sounding like other things, but we were really into hearing new things. Mike Mills from REM was huge for me. I kind of already played in a similar way, which was less of a root note approach and more of a "lead bass" approach.

Dan: Brian was getting into the Cocteau Twins records, and I think you can hear that influence in his guitar playing around that time.

Keith: That was a band that I was really into, and Brian really took to them, which was cool.

Brian: What a great band. Just the way Elizabeth Fraser's voice interacted with Robin Guthrie's guitars. Just amazing. They *definitely* influenced some of my guitar tones at the time.

One of the most notable differences in this album from previous recordings is the guitar sound, which has much to do with a unique piece of equipment that would become a key part of Die Kreuzen's later output.

Butch Vig: You'll have to ask Brian about this but, if I recall, he had this guitar that ran in stereo. I think he had it going to two different amps that were EQ'ed differently.

Brian: It was a Kramer Ripley that had this Bartolini stereo pickup in it. You could pan each string hard left, right, or centered. There were six pan-pots on the guitar so you could really do some interesting stuff to the stereo image. I had two Marshall half-stacks and used one as the wet

Brian pictured with his stereo-output Kramer Ripley guitar live in 1988. Very few of these guitars were manufactured, and its unique features greatly contributed to the band's expansive sound during their later years. Photo: Barbara Herring.

channel and the other as the dry channel and then panned the strings just a bit, and that's what really gave the guitars that distinct sound.

Butch Vig: That guitar gave them this giant 3-D kind of sound. Some of the songs on the record weren't double-tracked; we just cut them with him playing the stereo guitar live because it gave it a similar effect, just a really wide sound. We didn't need to go back and overdub more guitars. No one I knew was doing that at the time.

Brian: Rick [Canzano] had a difficult time understanding what we wanted out of the mix. Butch kept pushing me to push the guitars up louder in the mix, and I was hesitant because there were spots I wasn't happy with. In retrospect, they're fine. I think at the time, me being a perfectionist got in the way of us having an even better mix.

Keith: That's one thing we got from Butch—once you're done recording, just leave it for a little while so that you're not burned out on it. Maybe get a cassette as a reference or something but leave it for a few weeks. That way, when you come back to mix it, it'll be more realistic. That's the same reason why he never used huge reference monitors in the studio. He was all about presenting things in a way that was accurate. That was great advice.

There were some "live" mixes on there—like, if it required more than what Butch could do at once, we'd all be in the control room with our hands on the faders helping with the mix.

By early 1988, the album was complete but, unlike their previous releases which were released not long after their completion, the album that would become *Century Days* was delayed by design and layout issues.

Keith: I had met this guy that had done some photo work that I liked and wanted him to do some work on the *Century Days* layout. This was when digital photography was completely brand new.

Dan: I remember that guy being like, "Digital photos, dude. It's the future."

Keith: His contribution just took so much longer than we anticipated, which in turn delayed the release of the album. In retrospect it was totally stupid and not worth it.

Brian: It was something they, like . . . shot the image as a video and then took a photo of the video? It was really bizarre and took a long time. It ended up as a photo with our heads coming out of a volcano or something. That was fuckin' dumb.

Keith: I hold myself responsible for that. We knew we wanted something different and by the time he finished the photo it was really down to the wire. I don't think any of us were really over the moon about it, but it was something different to open up and de-seed your weed on [laughs].

The image in question appears in the album's gatefold. Photography-related obstacles aside, though, the visual presentation of *Century Days* was as labored over as the music. The advancements in both songwriting and production were matched by their visual collaborator and art director, Richard Kohl, who was seemingly operating on the same wavelength as the band. Just as the band was continuing to progress and experiment on a sonic level, Kohl's stunning visual style also moved forward, resulting in a sleeve that not only complements the music but also mirrors its own depth and complexity.

Richard Kohl: I always thought that with each release they just kept getting better. They just sent me a tape as they always did. I listened to the music a lot and paid close attention. They were going to new areas, and it was inspirational to me in creating the art and ideas would come to me. I just wanted the imagery to convey the same energy as the music. I had a lot of fun with that record cover and spent a lot of time on it.

Xeroxing was really fun and easy back then, and you could play around with images like that. A lot of images I'd use were things I saw in the newspaper. I'd save stuff like that all the time; I had a file full of stuff like that. For the *Century Days* art, it's all xeroxes that I either enlarged or shrunk down and then cut it all up and reassembled and rearranged it. Some of it literally went through paper shredders and I would space the images out.

It's really offbeat imagery. I had this broken alarm clock, and I took it apart and xeroxed the clock face a few times. There were a lot of Cold War images in there too. I seem to recall this photo of these two Soviet jet-fighter pilots that were modeling these new helmets or something like that? There's also some imagery from the White Night Riots in 1979 after the assassination of Harvey Milk and George Moscone. It was intense—people rioted and torched all the cop cars—and when I saw it I just thought that it was some real provocative imagery; I really liked it a lot. I tried to make it subtle, but it's there. There's a lot of weird energy in the artwork on that cover.

It was kind of like a puzzle in that I would keep taking it apart and re-assembling it. To get that color, I was taking it to the photo lab where I worked, just driving those people crazy with all this shit [laughs].

When it finally saw a release in July 1988, *Century Days* both looked and sounded like nothing else Die Kreuzen had done previously. Boasting a full-spectrum sonic upgrade from Butch Vig and a fluorescent gatefold sleeve, *Century Days* showed the band evolving on multiple levels.

For all of its obvious differences, though, there was still something familiar about the album. Though a considerable step forward from *October File* (and quite a drastic leap from the first album), *Century Days* was still very much a Die Kreuzen album—emotionally complex, shrouded in mystery, and not easy to pigeon-hole. Much as one could hear elements of the self-titled album on *October File*, *Century Days* shares a handful of sonic similarities with *October File*, while still moving the band's songwriting forward.

The album opener "Earthquakes" hints at what's to come with its sharp balance of melody and aggression. In the same way that the echoed reverb trails of "Man in the Trees" introduced the *October File* album, "Earthquakes" arrives like a slowly accelerating car. Tunison's drums give way to Egeness's warped atonal chords, manipulated by his guitar's tremolo arm. Brammer's driving bass completes the instrumental foundation, and by the time Kubinski's first vocal lines hit it's clear to anyone this could only be Die Kreuzen. The aggression, darkness, and tension of the band's previous releases are all still here, but they're juxtaposed with a refined melodic sensibility and midtempo approach that give its darker elements a brighter contrast, creating a push-pull dynamic that the band would continue to explore for years to come. Savvy listeners can hear "Earthquakes" and recognize that, if played faster, it would bear a close resemblance to the more ominous moments on *October File*.

"Lean into It" finds the band moving further into the melodic tilt of songs like "Cool Breeze," its clean, driving jangle recalling the sounds of early REM and Echo and the Bunnymen. On the surface, the track sounds sunnier than most Die Kreuzen tracks, but a darker undercurrent runs throughout Kubinski's vocal performance. The emotional core of Die Kreuzen exposes

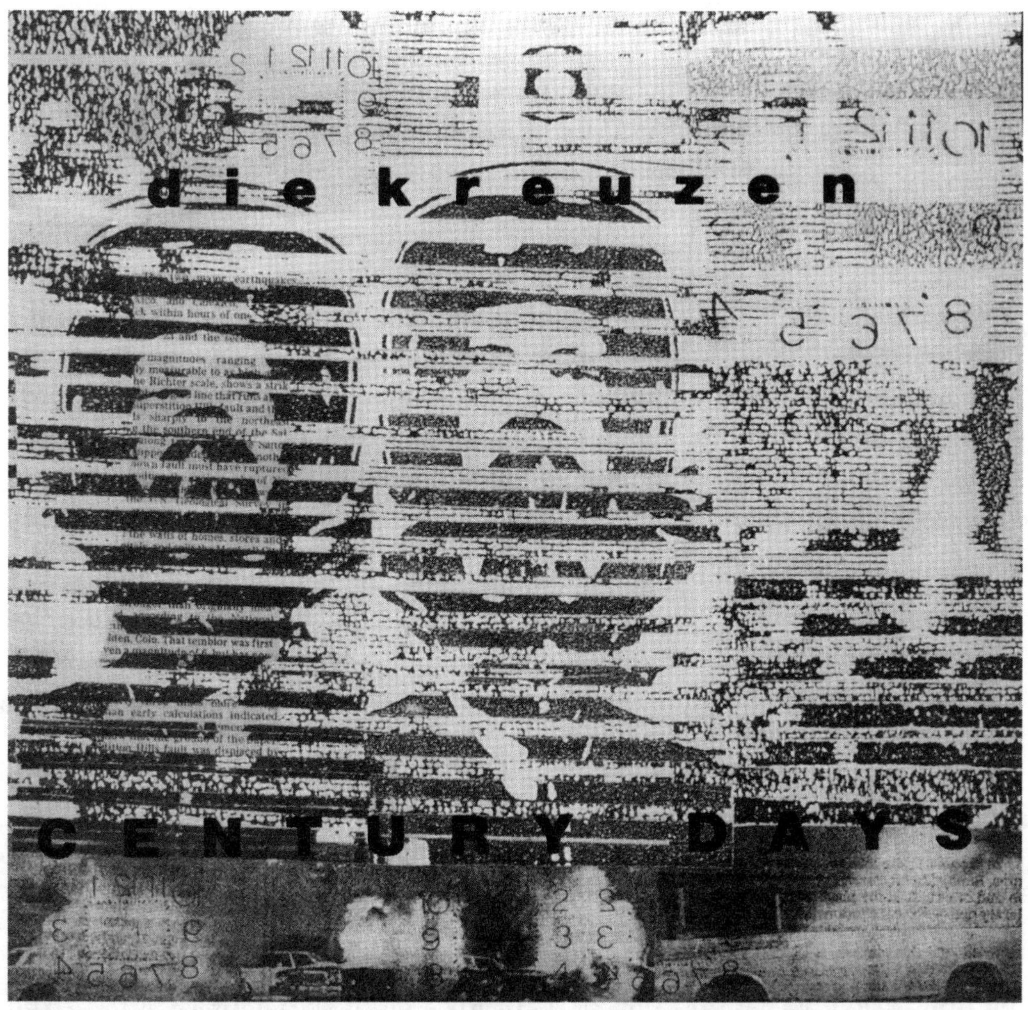

Matching the album's progressive sound, the *Century Days* album art featured hazy layers of photocopied images by Richard Kohl.

itself in different ways throughout their career, and "Lean into It" is but one example of Kubinski's performance steering the song's mood.

While many of the album's tracks show the band's growth as songwriters and musicians, the band never strays too far from their origins. At their core, Die Kreuzen were still a punk band and, no matter how melodic some of the album's songs leaned, there was still plenty of material that held true to the punk ethos of writing music that was aggressive and challenging.

"The Bone," while slower in tempo than anything on the self-titled album, is very much from the same lineage as that recording. The ominous terror and anguish of Kubinski's vocals that are hallmarks of the Die Kreuzen catalog take center stage here. His signature shriek as present as ever, Kubinski howls between bits of maniacal laughter to a 6/8 groove that results in a track that's as terrifying as it is intriguing.

"Bitch Magnet" is an abstract and deconstructed take on the hardcore punk of their early output. Kubinski screams and howls alongside the horns of the Crusties' Tim Cole. Though a horn arrangement would often lend to a song's accessibility, in this case the horns only reinforce the track's more ominous elements.

"Stomp" draws on Die Kreuzen's penchant for odd time signatures as explored on tracks like "Conditioned." While "Conditioned" sounded more like progressive post-hardcore, "Stomp" is perhaps the most straightforward rock 'n' roll song Die Kreuzen ever wrote, and even then it's still in the relatively uncommon time signature of 7/8. Employing the horn section once again, the use of horns on the song was a nod to the 1971 Rolling Stones track "Bitch."

In the same way that "Cool Breeze" stood apart from most of *October File*, especially when compared to the debut album, "Number Three" is one of the more noticeable left turns on *Century Days*. Its molasses-slow tempo gives the band room to expand and explore their more psychedelic side, driven by Egeness's swirling stereo guitars. It's dreamy yet unnerving, never letting up for six-plus minutes. Previous tracks were about endurance and speed, but "Number Three" is the opposite, focusing on patience and atmoshpere. If *October File*'s album art looks like the sound of "Man in the Trees," then *Century Days*' album art looks like the sound of "Number Three."

Of all the albums in the Die Kreuzen discography, *Century Days* is easily the most stylistically broad of them, placing slow psychedelic dirges alongside jangle-pop homages. Die Kreuzen's sonic language was growing in both directions. Nothing was being abandoned, but the band's penchant for melody was finding its way to the forefront in the songwriting. In the same way that writing tight and fast hardcore is an art, so is crafting a song with memorable melodies, and it's rare to find an act who was able to succeed at both. Die Kreuzen's first notable attempt at doing so resulted in the album's most hook-laden song, "Elizabeth."

Rhythmically driving with a soaring chorus, "Elizabeth" showed a new addition to the band's color palette that plenty of their contemporaries were unable to obtain. "Elizabeth" is one of *Century Days'* brightest moments but, much like "Lean into It," it's an emotionally multi-dimensional song, delivering bright and hopeful elements with an equal dose of bittersweet melancholia. There's a term in Portuguese—"saudade"—that loosely translates as a feeling of longing, melancholy, and nostalgia. The word appears frequently in Brazilian music, specifically bossa nova, and is something that is much more easily felt than explained. There's no easy translation for it in the English language but, as a feeling, "Elizabeth" feels like "saudade."

Butch Vig: To me, "Elizabeth" sounded like it could have been written by some of those early 4AD Records bands. I could definitely hear more of the English influences on that song especially.

Neko Case: When I think of Die Kreuzen, I always think about Bad Brains because they both decided to stop fighting melodies and really let the melodies come out. I don't want to say that melody just belongs to women either. Because I love super-fast hardcore as much as anybody, but there had to be more to it than just that. There had to be some imperfection or melody to give it something else.

Century Days was great. I wasn't at all disappointed in the fact that they didn't repeat themselves. It still sounded like them, but there were all of these new sounds on there too. They dealt with really sharp and angular sounds but made them really beautiful, and not a lot of artists can do that. They did that a lot more on *Century Days,* but there was a wider variety of them. And it was all so well curated, this really jagged but beautiful sound.

Bob Nastanovich: My favorite songs of theirs are all on *Century Days.* To me, that's their best work; I can listen to any song on there. Their talents were being displayed in a far better way once they branched out, and *Century Days* just does a great job of showing that. I was in college then, and that music just went so well with our cheap-weed and cheap-beer lifestyle. We all sort of bonded on that. I think all the early members of Silver Jews—Die Kreuzen was a band we all loved, especially David Berman. He loved Die Kreuzen. He loved every element of them.

Without Butch's production, I don't think it would've been as great as it is. I think they wanted it to be dramatic like those 4AD records. It was so gothy and heavy, it was almost frightening in a way.

Nathan Larson: *Century Days* is awesome. The way "Earthquakes" just comes in, it just sounds great. It gave me the same feeling as "Man in the Trees." You can hear that stereo guitar sound—it sounds so special. Like, even just the feedback, it's such a beautiful tone. They had this great way of introducing songs, where they'd introduce elements individually. With that song there's a drum intro, and then the feedback comes in, and then the bass comes in high for a bit and then drops, and it's just so well done and thoughtfully arranged.

"Stomp" is really rad. Their use of horns on that song is so interesting. For me, those horns hit me in the same way that a lot of New York fractal jazz stuff hit me, stuff like the Lounge Lizards or John Zorn. The horns aren't sitting there doing pads—they have their own weird part to it. It was super-arty and jazzy—it felt good. It didn't feel like Jane's Addiction or something—it was this really cool, noir kind of thing they were doing.

Even that cover of "Halloween" is so cool—it made so much sense for them. The way they wove all those parts together, it felt like such a perfect encapsulation of what they were doing. *Century Days* just delivered so hard on the promise of *October File*. It's all just very beautifully executed.

Jon Wurster: All the experimentation with melody that they had started to do with *October File*, they took it even further on *Century Days*. I feel like "Elizabeth" was the crystallization of all those elements coming together. That could've been on REM's *Life's Rich Pageant*. Like, yeah, a few years earlier he had that really great hardcore scream, but with "Elizabeth" Dan proved that he really was a versatile singer.

Dan: I had heard "Birthday" by the Sugarcubes and was really intrigued by what Björk was doing vocally in the song. The way she was using her voice in the song was very unique and very musical and I really liked it.

Later that week at rehearsal we were writing "Elizabeth," and I think that "Birthday" definitely had an influence on the way I approached the vocals for that song.

By the late '80s, MTV was as big of a promotional platform as radio and, while getting a video to the channel was no small feat, both the band and Corey saw potential for "Elizabeth" as a single. They decided to make a video for the track, though the process of doing so proved to be more difficult than it seemed.

Corey Rusk: "Elizabeth" . . . this was sort of the beginning of that time period where on rare occasions a record on an indie label could get real airplay on radio and MTV and have it make a difference. We had no budget to make a video like that, but I thought that song was amazing; to me it felt like one of those songs where if people just heard it they would love it, so I wanted to do everything that we could to get people to hear it.

I rented a 16mm camera and they found some kids who had some in with this cool theater. I don't think it was abandoned, but it definitely wasn't operational. We rented a bunch of lights and spent the day with them on stage performing it over and over again.

Keith: We shot the video for "Elizabeth" in this theater like an hour south of Milwaukee in Racine or Kenosha, somewhere around there. We set up the theater with all these lights and stuff, and it looked great.

Corey Rusk: I swear there was a boombox on stage playing the song. They didn't want to just be miming, and they actually played along with it.

Keith: For whatever reason, we were dead set on the video synching up with the music. We later went to edit it at Southern Studios while we were on tour in London. We sat in that place for almost two fucking days trying to get it to work when we could have been out sightseeing or whatever.

Dan: We didn't have any film clapper or anything to help us easily sync the audio up to the video. We just had all this reference footage, on VHS tapes, and it was just the picture—there was no sound at all. We sat there and, like, tried to read my lips or tried to see whose hands were where. "Oh, that's the chorus! Let's see if we can put this part in." That's how we put that whole video together.

Keith: What any sensible band would have done is realize that no one was paying that close attention to it.

One of the most interesting things about *Century Days* comes in the form of its closing track, a cover of the theme to John Carpenter's 1978 slasher classic *Halloween*. A strange cover choice, no doubt, as up until this point the band had only ever released original compositions on their albums. More involved listening will reveal that the song's iconic piano line sounds not unlike some of the riffs on *Century Days*, most notably its off-kilter 5/4 time signature. Interestingly, the band's relationship to the song goes back further than one may realize.

Dan: Early on—like, even prior to the first album—we were asked by these young skate kids to play their high school dance. I think we had to play like two half-hour or forty-five-minute sets? For us, though, we were just like, "Man, what are we gonna do?" I think we did an extended version of "Interstellar Overdrive" and an extended version of "All White." I think we maybe even played that twice, once at the beginning and again at the end [laughs]. In trying to find stuff that we could do to fill up the sets, we did this cover version of the theme from "Halloween," so we decided to open with it.

Years later, someone reminded us about how we used to play that, and we decided to bring it back. I just remember Keith and Brian finding the chords and figuring out the arrangement. It was really fun in the studio because we kinda did it as a free jam. We had a loose structure to it because you had to know the changes and stuff, but it was free and loose and fun. All that screaming and stuff was great to go in and cut loose. I think Butch even flipped the reels over so we could have some sounds that were going backwards.

The variety of sounds, moods, and emotions on *Century Days* went far beyond the average hardcore punk band. To call it punk, hardcore, college rock, or otherwise would be to only focus on one of the album's many elements. Much like *October File* before it, *Century Days* is very much a post-hardcore record and, while not obviously similar, it fits comfortably alongside other releases of the era like Hüsker Dü's *Zen Arcade*, Slint's *Tweez*, and Dinosaur Jr.'s *You're Living All over Me*.

Keith: I remember giving the finished record to Corey and him not really saying much of anything—not in a bad way or anything, just that he wasn't surprised by the new material because he had seen us play those songs a few times already.

Dan: I think the real shock for him was when we submitted *October File.* After that he knew that we were going to keep moving forward.

Keith: After that record he didn't bat an eyelash, really. His logic was, "Well, I signed you because you didn't sound like anyone else, so I can hardly complain about it now." There were a few bands on Touch and Go that tended to repeat themselves; like, they released a third record, and it sounded the same as the two before it. Corey was more concerned about signing bands that were interesting. He didn't really care whether it would sell or not, but for the most part that worked to his advantage.

Still, the band was prepared for pushback from the fanbase. The musicians who created hardcore punk in the early '80s were often taking influences from a variety of sources, though it may have been difficult to hear. As has been noted, the members of Die Kreuzen always had eclectic tastes, even prior to their formation of the band. It's interesting to observe that a specific faction of the fanbase cherished bands so much, but not enough to allow them to grow. While this is due in part to the bands having broader taste than their fans, it's still an interesting concept, to hold a desire for a creative arrested development.

Nonetheless, for the fans who didn't understand the direction that Die Kreuzen was continuing to move in, there were plenty of new fans who were drawn towards the new material who may have been deterred by their earlier output.

Butch Vig: I love it when bands progress. As a listener but also as a producer, that's exciting. I don't want a band or an artist to have one sound and stay there, and I think most artists feel the same way. A lot of times in the underground, the audiences want them to stay the same and play the same songs at the same clubs for the same people, but no artist wants to do that. Most artists want to continue moving forward and make music that reflects the present.

John Reis: This happens with every type of music including hardcore—you get these dummies who are only interested in hearing that one thing and nothing else.

Even someone like me, who would've loved to hear another version of the first LP again, I realized that this was a band who wanted to change and do something different. I like this band, and they exposed me to something new, with all kinds of new possibilities. They showed me that you could actually make music like that. To me, why wouldn't I allow them to do that for me again with something different? If you like someone's art, if they make something that you think is incredible, at least give them that fucking license to continue to grow. Realize that if you don't like it now you may like it later. Maybe you're just not ready for it.

They were ahead of their time with that first record, so why wouldn't they be ahead of their time as they continued to evolve? People got away from hardcore because the limitations weren't in the music—the limitations were in the role that people thought the music should play in their identity.

Kim Thayil: *Century Days* didn't grab me the way *October File* did, and I think it might have been because I was framing it in relation to *October File*. As an album, though, *Century Days* is a beautiful title and package. The thing that grabbed me most about it was "Number Three." I just love that song; it really stuck with me. Beautiful, ambient, dark, but floral. The whole thing just blossoms and is so full of color even though it's also so moody. That's a fuckin' super-cool song.

Century Days was interesting because there's things on there that felt more in line with what was happening in Minneapolis at the time, like the Replacements and Soul Asylum. With Die Kreuzen being this great hardcore band that eventually turned into this arty progressive band from the future, those elements are totally there on tracks like "Stomp" and "Number Three." There's stuff on there that maybe feels like bar punk, and hearing Die Kreuzen do that was new for me. It wasn't something I'd expect from them.

Justin Trosper: The first record of theirs I heard was *Century Days* around the time it came out. I think I probably heard it through college radio.

I think back then, everything was still being discovered. Back then amongst my friend group, one person would buy a record and the rest of us would tape it. We were a pretty open-minded group; we weren't true hardcore kids who only listened to the loud and fast stuff. *Century Days* came out right when the Sub Pop stuff was coming out, and to me it really made a connection to some of those kinds of bands that we were starting to see in Olympia and Seattle. That record still holds a lot of water for me.

Die Kreuzen were experimenting with a lot of things but still keeping a strong toehold in their hardcore punk ethos. Even early on, they were

Die Kreuzen perform live in 1987 (possibly at the Metro). Photo courtesy of Die Kreuzen. Photographer unknown.

Keith tears it up on stage at Stache's in Columbus, Ohio, in 1988. Photo: Jay Brown.

going outside of the box, that they weren't just doing this garage punk type thing. You can just tell they aspired to something a little bit more evolved. Even the title—*Century Days*? What does that mean? The lyrical content was way more introverted and emotional, not obvious, more poetic license. People don't call bands like Die Kreuzen and Hüsker Dü "emo," but in a way they're kind of the ideal version of that. It's the real raw deal.

There was all this stuff in the latter half of the '80s that was all over the place. Along with the super punk stuff, there were also these kinda out there, more art-damaged things like Butthole Surfers. The first wave of hardcore punk was over, and all these people had moved onto doing these things that were weirder. Die Kreuzen was riding that threshold between this hardcore sound but also leaning into things like hard rock and metal in a way that wasn't at all retro, it was very forward-thinking. It just felt like this was where the music was going.

Upon its release, the press commended the band for their progression. *CMJ* called it "one of the supreme achievements by an American indie rock band," praising both the album's musicianship and its upgraded production. *Option* wrote, "[T]heir third and best LP is a constantly surprising outing that melds post punk mewlings and softer, semi-acoustic sounds into a whole without pretension or scattershot eclectism. . . . *Century Days* will prove to be one of the year's best releases." It undoubtedly challenged listeners but rewarded those who took the time to sit with the record's sub-hour runtime.

The challenging nature of their music made Die Kreuzen difficult to categorize; they were aggressive but also melodic. In 1988, the concept of combining the two opposites was still uncharted territory. Michael Alago at Elektra continued to keep in touch with the band and see them when he could, but eventually the band started to wonder if they would ever start talking seriously with the label.

Dan: We stayed in touch with Michael. Every time we played New York, he'd always be there. He'd always take us out to eat and have new Cure and Housemartins cassettes for us. I remember one day, all of us had a little extra to drink and we were sitting with him outside the club. I think it was Brian who just kinda asked Michael, "Hey, what's going on? Are you gonna sign us?" and I believe he said something to the effect of, "I think you guys are just too far ahead of your time. I love you guys, but I just don't know quite what to do with you."

Michael Alago: I recall one of them asking if Elektra was going to sign them or not. Ultimately, I didn't sign them because I felt it would have been totally unfair to put them in a corporate environment where I was the only one rooting for them. When you work for a major label, after a while you know the dos and don'ts of the company, and at that point I just didn't think it would work.

Marilynn Mee (radio programmer, WLZR, Milwaukee): If you were someone who really appreciated music, how could you not like Die Kreuzen? At the same time, how could you go to a major radio station in 1988 and expect those people to understand it, much less make a case for them to get airplay? At the time, you needed to sound like something really specific, and Die Kreuzen walked this line of being both heavy and melodic. I heard record-industry people say things like, "I wouldn't know what to do with them," because it was beyond categorization. For people who worked at major labels, it was difficult for them to comprehend and pin down. They were the one band that to me felt like they couldn't care less about getting a record deal. Fuck being commercial—they were just gonna be Die Kreuzen. I supported them because I just *knew* they were something really important.

Touring was more than just a means of promoting the band's newest release. It also gave them the opportunity to try out new songs they were working on. Always looking forward, their audiences weren't always receptive to what the band chose to play.

Dan: We'd always test out new material in our live sets. As soon as a song was done, we'd put it into the set. Sometimes people were into the new material and other times they'd shout at us: "Play something fast! Thrash!"

Greg Anderson: You'd go and see the band in hopes of hearing songs that you knew, but the band was already past that. You'd see them and they'd be like a year ahead of where you were, playing songs off a record that hadn't been released yet. Today, it's more about playing the hits, playing songs people know. For some people, it's about celebrating the past, like playing a specific album in its entirety. As a fan of the band, it's great to see that, but at the same time I miss when bands took more chances and tried out different ideas, regardless of what the audience thought. To me, that always felt more like, "This is what we do, and we're going to do it on our own terms," rather than pandering to what the audience wanted. That was definitely something Die Kreuzen did—like, always. I miss that; it's way more exciting and far less predictable.

Jon Wurster: It was so hard for a band like that to break out of that umbrella of having been a hardcore band. You could progress—and I don't think any band from that era progressed more than Die Kreuzen did—but you still had this stigma of being a hardcore band. I remember driving to see them on the *Century Days* tour and there couldn't have been more than seventy or eighty people there. I just remember them being great.

Erik is such a great drummer. Those parts on all those records are really well thought out and well executed. I hope he gets more credit than he does [now]. All their elements worked together in a way that was unlike anyone else. When I saw them, I remember being really impressed with Erik. He used everything so tastefully. He played a lot, and he would hit everything, but it was never too much That's an incredible feat for a drummer—to be kinda busy but not have it be too much. His patterns were super-cool and just watching him was almost like a ballet.

Keith's playing combined with his Rickenbacker is such a distinct sound. Keith is just one of the greatest . . . rock 'n' rollers of all time. I'd put him right up there with Tom Peterson or Steve Nieve or Peter Buck, any of those guys who just look fabulous while playing. He was meant to play a Rickenbacker guitar onstage. Brian's guitar-playing for a lot of their career sounded really processed, but in a good way. And of course, Dan—you couldn't mistake his voice for anyone else. By then, I remember feeling that hardcore was kind of over. I can't imagine what the guys in Die Kreuzen felt like at that point. Beyond over it, probably, and so ready to do their own thing and see who comes to it. Having to show up and play with a bunch of local thrash bands but being miles ahead of that in your own headspace. I can't imagine what that must've been like.

Marilynn Mee: The first time I saw Die Kreuzen, I remember being so mesmerized. I had never seen a band with that sort of stage presence or that sort of energy onstage. I never saw a band who dressed like them. Everything about them was different than what was happening at the time. They just looked so cool, but it was so effortless. So many bands around that time were putting on their eyeliner and their spandex and teasing their hair and whatever else, and the music was just about trying to get chicks and Die Kreuzen just felt so far beyond that. They had this air about them that they didn't give a fuck if you got them or not. You could just tell that it was clearly all about the music to them. And the funny thing was, the timeslot wasn't the best, I think it was like earlier during

Above: Die Kreuzen live in action in Dillsburg, Pennsylvania, 1987.

Below: Die Kreuzen perform in a shadowy haze in Dillsburg, Pennsylvania, 1987. Photos: Scott Lubic.

the daytime, but they played as if there were ten thousand people there watching them. It was so interesting and such a breath of fresh air.

Bob Nastanovich: If you saw that band in a club that held 400 people, you would have thought that you were at some huge European rock festival. It was just really powerful and dramatic and they hit hard. It was hard rock—it was so powerful. We always kind of felt that we were Die Kreuzen fans after the fact, and we felt like people turned their backs on them when they were really starting to get great. People just couldn't handle the dramatic transition.

If you were standing there watching them, they were just intense, just completely zoned in. They'd play a set like that in front of smaller crowds, but it was fantastic. I remember seeing them play to, like, eighty people, and they were great, and they played great, and I'd always be thinking, "Why isn't this band playing arenas?" because to me they *were* that good. If you compare 2008-era My Morning Jacket to 1988-era Die Kreuzen, there's no comparison as to who the better band is. Die Kreuzen just had this *massive* sound.

Among the many shows Die Kreuzen played during the *Century Days* era, they got the opportunity to play with one of the band's biggest key influences, the Ramones. Unlike some of their favorite acts, the Ramones remained faithful to their initial thesis of shorter, louder, and faster. Whether it was pandering to their audience or otherwise, Ramones fans knew exactly what they wanted. Unfortunately for Die Kreuzen, *Century Days* wasn't exactly the ideal album for most Ramones die-hards.

Keith: We played with the Ramones at L'Amour, which was, like, a metal venue in the middle of the Hasidic section of Brooklyn. It was pretty big, probably about a couple thousand capacity. The place was packed. The thing with the Ramones, though, was that no matter who it was that was opening, the people were there just to see the Ramones, no one else. Just a thankless task really, but we loved the Ramones.

Brian: Oh god, I remember the crowd was throwing shit at us.

Dan: We were playing and everyone in the audience was just booing us incessantly. Joey was standing on the side of the stage just watching and laughing. Eventually he said to me, "Come here, come here," and called me over. I thought he was gonna help me out or tell me something that'll make the situation better or whatever. Instead, he just handed me the "Gabba

Gabba Hey" sign. He just looked at me and said, "Just go ahead, go for it." I go out there with the sign and we're playing, like, "Elizabeth" or something. The crowd got even more mad and started yelling even more [laughs].

Keith: I think on one side of the sign it said "Gabba Gabba Hey" and on the other side it said "Fuck You." It was bad enough with the "Gabba Gabba Hey" side; when he flipped it around the crowd got even worse. The Ramones were great, though. Their "smoke machine" was just a bunch of cigarettes duct taped to a piece of wood. I remember seeing that and thinking, "Wow, that's pretty clever," until they lit the thing, and it was like someone jamming an entire pack of cigarettes in your face.

Brian: After the show we went down to the numbered streets [the Lower East Side of New York City] with Joey. I remember there being some dudes with guns there. Joey eventually passed out on the couch and all of us kinda decided that we should just get the fuck out of there as quickly as possible.

As the band continued to move away from the traditional hardcore punk of the debut album, the band wanted to play for audiences who were more open-minded and interested in progressive music. This included their first ever tour overseas, which covered parts of continental Europe in October of 1988. The continually positive press they received via magazines like *NME* and *Melody Maker* certainly helped, as did playing with similarly-minded artists. More adventurous post-hardcore acts began to give the band the opportunity to play for more receptive audiences. Hot off the heels of the release of their *Daydream Nation* album, Sonic Youth looked to Die Kreuzen and Laughing Hyenas as main support for their tour, which covered both North America and Europe.

Keith: We had been friends with them [Sonic Youth] for a while at that point, and once they got bigger they would get in touch with us and have us play strings of shows with them. A lot of the time it would be them, us, and the Laughing Hyenas. We did a few tours like that over the space of a couple of years.

The people who went to see them were great. They wouldn't just show up like five minutes before Sonic Youth went on; they would be there for the entire show and watch all of the bands. People were into the whole spectrum of sounds, and that was great for us.

Dan: It was great to have people actually watch us and be into what we were doing instead of yelling, "Play faster, goddammit!" or "Get a haircut!" at us.

A flyer for one of the many shows on the Sonic Youth / Die Kreuzen / Laughing Hyenas tour, 1988, a.k.a. the "Monsters of Hardcore" tour.

Keith: For me it was great because I got to see Sonic Youth and the Hyenas a bunch of times and both of them put on really great live shows.

Thurston Moore: We did this tour with them and the Laughing Hyenas, and that tour was a real nexus point for us historically. That will always be a really important part of our history. For me, they were just these two bands that were within and coming out of hardcore but doing something else. It wasn't like going out on the road with the Necros; these bands sort of had a progressive attitude about what they were doing. It was this super cool tour. The Hyenas were coming out of Negative Approach, but they were doing this really cool take on the Birthday Party and some other things . . . and you had John Brannon singing in this hyper wail.

I really liked both of those bands, but Steve was really the strongpoint of that because he knew all of them from having played with them in the Crucifucks. I just liked this idea of having this gang on the road.

Die Kreuzen and the Hyenas together, that was a tough crew. They were gambling and throwing dice on the street and stuff, but first and foremost they were there for the music. They weren't looking for trouble. No one had any money anyway.

Brian: I think we were at the Italian border, and we couldn't cross it because they closed it off at night. We were stuck in a motel room right next to the border crossing and just sat in the room and played craps.

Lou Barlow: We did some shows on that tour, but I almost remember nothing of that era from Dinosaur [Jr.] because I was such a nervous wreck at the time. Like, even just being around Sonic Youth, I'm sure I was deeply starstruck when I had to talk to them, which didn't even make sense because they were very friendly and kind to us. We hung out all the time, but I couldn't really speak to them. Adding Die Kreuzen into the mix, I can just imagine being backstage and me thinking, like, "Oh my god, Die Kreuzen are behind that door," not even being able to be in their presence [laughs].

Brian: There were a lot of people at those shows, and I never would've guessed that that many people would be interested in a band like Sonic Youth, especially after the fact. To see them start to flourish at that time was really cool.

Thurston Moore: I think the biggest show we played on that tour was

Brian performs live on stage with Sonic Youth's Thurston Moore on tour, 1988. Photo courtesy of Die Kreuzen. Photographer unknown.

probably at the Ritz in New York. At the time there was this big tour with Van Halen and the Scorpions called the "Monsters of Rock" tour, and I remember Lyle Hysen from Das Damen saying that ours was the "Monsters of Hardcore" tour. Like, even though we weren't hardcore, that was where hardcore had grown into at that point. The fact that many people in New York had come to see Sonic Youth, Die Kreuzen, and Laughing Hyenas kinda blew his mind, 'cause, like, hardcore had always been just, like, twenty guys in a room circle-pitting. It was just really exciting and super-fun. ●

NEVER ENOUGH AND ALWAYS TOO MUCH

Greetings!Back again(for a month at least).A good time was had by all on the last tour;the van held up and we missed the hurricane!Thanks again to everyone involved.Rock'n'roll!

Digital Mania Dept.

As everyone prepares to enter the 90's,we take the monumentous step of releasing our first two LP's on one ultra-long-playing CD!Complete with fantastic booklet(including new photos).Just in time for Christmas!Bargain city,folks!!!

Gone and(apparently)
All-But-Forgotten Dept.

ROCK HOTEL PRESENTS
HAWKWIND
Die Kreuzen
Dreamspeak
THURS ■ SEPT 28 ■ 8PM SHOW ...... Note New Date!
$14.50 ADV/$15.50 DAY

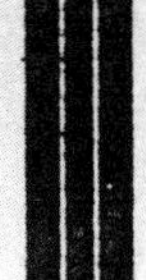

As might be judged from the headline,the turnout for the triumphant return of Hawkwind to these shores was less than staggering, but they still managed to rock us to our shoes with songs such as 'Hashish'Fun,fun,fun.

GREENPEACE
P.O. Box 3720, Washington, D.C. 20007

The legendary Holland Tunnel Motel.Always a little on the seedy side,it seems to have taken a definite turn for the worse,and we are forced to withdraw our coveted Die Kreuzen seal of approval.Yes,the rooms really do look like that.

Continental Voyagers Dept.

Yes, we're going back to Europe! Hooray! We'll be departing on December 4th, not to return until January 17th. We'll be visiting England, Switzerland, Holland, Italy, Yugoslavia, Germany and Austria. More details on this as we get them.

We actually did visit here on our last trip to Pittsburgh, and it's as amazing as its name would suggest!

The Bar is Open!

Extraordinarily

Perceptive

Criticism Dept.

Kreuzen Spans Three Decades

Instructing you to play the studio side at 45, comprised of two songs "Gone Away" and "Seasons of Wither" pretty well sums up Die Kreuzen's departure from their early thrash roots, from hell and back again on the latest 45, *Gone Away*. The numbers sound more like Ozzy than Milwaukee's evil-doers that done good, and I was surprised to hear that Dan Kubinski can sing like a regular rocker after screaming for so many years continuously. These works should be liked by the kids that grew up with MTV, but may disappoint those that want their teeth to chatter and then shatter.

When you cue up the next side and forget to reset the RPM, as I did, you immediately think, yes, they still really cook. Then returning to 33, Kubinski sounds like Roger Waters!

Each subsequent ditty on the live side, savors and teases, with more high energy guitar and fast drum, working toward frenzy. It drives faster and faster until the soul of old Die Kreuzen is resurrected. The psychedelic trance that "The Trees Magnet," evokes is the strongest field of flux density and last of the live selections. It leaves you hanging, hungry for more, out on a limb. It's the existential mourning of 1970s rock, the demonic buzzsaw and electricity of the 1980s with an eclectic eye to the 1990s for heavy metal.

—Jeff Worman

The Travellers' Friends Dept.

Die Kreuzen heartily endorses the following:

Records to watch for: <u>Badger A Go Go</u> compilation LP (Atomic); featuring a (slightly) alternative version of our take on 'Seasons...' plus lots of other great Milwaukee bands. <u>Wreck</u> 12" EP (Play It Again Sam); debut from a v. cool Chicago combo, featuring yours truly on bass. <u>Kevn Kinney</u> LP (Island); solo album from the Drivin'n'Cryin man. I've heard it, and it's fucking awesome. <u>Voivod</u> - <u>Nothingface</u> LP (MCA/Mechanic); The progression that I (if not legions of metal fans) hoped they'd make. Fab.

Die Kreuzen
P.O.Box 92181
Milwaukee, WI
53202

One of the many newsletters the band would send their fans over the course of a year. Pre-internet, this was an extremely important way for bands to directly communicate with their audiences.

Keith deep in the mist on stage at Bogart's in Cincinnati Ohio, c. 1987. Photo: Jay Brown

Gone Away, Pink Flag, and Mechanic Records

THE SHEER TERROR HEARD ON THE DEBUT ALBUM TOOK A back seat to something more melodic and nuanced on *Century Days*. Songs like "Elizabeth" and "Lean into It" showed that the band was capable of writing songs with a more melodic focus and stood apart from some of the album's other tracks, like the slow-burning psych jam "Number Three" or the ominous dirge "The Bone." By this point, Die Kreuzen was a band with a complex sound, and their albums reflected this. They had yet to write a song that highlighted everything they did well, but that was soon to change with a song called "Gone Away."

Dating back to 1988, "Gone Away" was a gorgeous portrait of the band showcasing nearly every facet of their sound. The band's knack for melodicism is presented at its finest here, yet the song still sounds unmistakably like Die Kreuzen, with Kubinski still finding an opportunity to use his complete vocal range. Sans the break-neck pace of the band's earlier material, "Gone Away" highlights nearly everything that the band did well and does so in the strongest way possible—a perfect distillation of the band's finest qualities in a razor-sharp three-and-a-half-minute tune. Arguably their single strongest songwriting achievement as a band, it makes perfect sense that the band decided to record and release the song as a stand-alone EP.

Keith: It seemed like it was taking us forever between records, and we were looking for a stopgap of sorts. Corey suggested we put out a single.

Brian: I think from doing "Seasons of Wither" cover, Aerosmith was an influence on "Gone Away." It was extremely cold out when I wrote that song. I can't remember if we did the photo shoot before or after we wrote that song, but we took some photos by the lakefront where everything was just frozen over, ice everywhere. I took that frozen feeling back to the practice space, sat down, and worked it out.

Keith: I came up with that bassline, and I just remember it was one of those instances where the next thing that everyone came up with just made the song better. It wasn't a completely formed song that one person wrote; it was really built up by all four of us together. When that happens, it's the greatest thing in the world.

Dan: It was this perfect coming together of everyone's abilities, each of our ribbons tying a bow.

Butch Vig: "Gone Away" was a fantastic song because it really had all these different elements within it. It was moody and dreamy and aggressive, but it also had this psychedelic feel at some points. It's just this really powerful and hooky song.

Dan: We worked on that song for a while, worked it out during practices, and it started to take shape. Then we went and recorded it, and really started to think about what we wanted it to be, hearing all the separate parts, thinking about what we wanted the vocals to sound like, all that.

Keith: I loved that song. I think it turned out great and it didn't sound even remotely like anything else we had done up to that point.

Dan: When it was done, I was at home a few days later, and it was quiet, so I took the cassette of it that Butch gave me and put it in my Walkman, put the headphones on, hit play, and started walking down the street.

The first album I always liked. *October File* was this weird mishmash, and at the time I wasn't really quite sure what it was. *Century Days* was somewhat more of that—still punk but with some weird psychedelia creeping in. I liked it, and I liked the creativity, but I didn't know what to make of it. When I hit play on "Gone Away" for that first time after finishing it, though, I couldn't believe that it was us, I really couldn't. When I heard what we had done, it was just like, "Wow, we've really done something here. We did it—we've made the kind of music that we'd want to listen to."

Corey Rusk: I totally thought that song could've been a hit. I thought that when I first heard it, and I still think that today. I was totally blown away by that song.

Jon Wurster: They just continued to show everyone what they were capable of. "Gone Away" was really just them continuing to move in that direction, showing everyone that they could write these really catchy songs.

Butch Vig: I think that song was a reason why they started getting more calls from major labels—it really showed the majors what their band was capable of. Had that song been on a major label, I think it's possible that it would've gotten a pretty big push and done well on college radio and alternative radio.

Erik: I think it's great—"Hey, look at this—we wrote a rock song in waltz time!" I think it turned out fantastic, right down to Richard's artwork.

Whether an album or single release, Die Kreuzen always considered every element of their recorded output before the ideas became a finished product. Working again with Richard Kohl, the single sleeve for "Gone Away" was, much like the music, unlike anything else they had done prior.

Richard Kohl: The "Gone Away" art was a painting that I did. I took a lot of watercolor classes that I enjoyed quite a bit. The idea was a big tombstone, kinda similar to the headstone on the *Cows and Beer* record. At that time, I was a production manager in an art studio, and we had to learn how to do all these faux finishes. I was playing around trying to make it look like marble or something. It's pretty dramatic. It was a nightmare for Corey to print that. They had to print that, even though it was all black and white—they had to print it in a dark grey and a black to give it that depth. It turned out fantastic.

Keith: Once again, we were like, "Let's do white vinyl and have the artwork fold out into a cross!" And we wonder where our royalties went [laughs].

The single also featured a cover version of "Seasons of Wither" by Aerosmith, a shadowy cut from their *Get Your Wings* album. Egeness's remark that the song had an influence on the writing of "Gone Away" makes sense here; at its core, "Seasons of Wither" feels like its spiritual sibling. Arpeggiated guitars and a subdued vocal performance allow the song to breathe and

Above: After shooting photos on the ice, the band began work on what eventually became the song "Gone Away." Photo: Ron Faiola.

Below: Richard Kohl's meticulously crafted sleeve for the "Gone Away" single, with the sleeve unfolding into the shape of a cross. The twelve-inch featured a different illustration in a similar style,

simmer within the somber and moody atmosphere. It's a patient song that, similar to "Gone Away," creates an environment with sound and gives the song a very vivid sense of location. Die Kreuzen's take on it is quite faithful to the original, further demonstrating Aerosmith's influence on the band.

By this point, the band had made a habit of not printing their lyrics in the liner notes, instead preferring listeners to make their own interpretations of what Kubinski was singing. This decision didn't prevent the music from making an impact on an emotional level, still landing with listeners in a meaningful way, conveying far more in its ambiguity than it would have with a clear lyrical explanation.

The decision to not include lyric sheets didn't prevent the music from making an impact, though. The instrumental performances and vocal delivery were so raw and real that the songs still landed with listeners on an emotional level. As a result, this allowed the songs to resonate with listeners in a meaningful and significant way, conveying far more in their ambiguity than they would have otherwise.

The band was always striving to give their listeners something new each time, and decided to release two different versions of the single-a two song seven-inch with "Gone Away" and "Seasons of Wither," and a longer twelve-inch EP with live tracks on the B side. For this release specifically, the band decided to record a gig in Milwaukee at the Odd Rock Café, on Kinnickinnic Avenue in the working-class Bay View neighborhood. In an era before Pro Tools, producing a great live recording was pretty much contingent on two things–solid performances and a skilled engineer. The band called on Butch Vig and Bill Stace to help capture the band's energetic live performances on tape.

Keith: We thought recording the live show was gonna be really easy, and the next thing you know, Butch and Bill Stace are down there [at the Odd Rock Café] running all these cables into the basement [laughs].

Butch Vig: That was kind of recorded by the seat of our pants. I can't remember if we did that on a four- or eight-track, but it was pretty crudely assembled. It wasn't anything state-of-the-art like the mobile recording trucks the Stones used or whatever—we just used what we had available to us. I remember it was just really haphazard and right before they started playing we were just like, "Okay, all the mics are working, everything is being recorded, so let's just go with it."

There really wasn't a lot of manipulation that I could do. It was just record the performances and try to finesse them a bit in the mixing process, but it ended up sounding great.

The resulting recordings of Die Kreuzen playing live at Milwaukee's Odd Rock Café showed just how strong of a live act Die Kreuzen was. Pulling six tracks from *October File* and *Century Days*, the live tracks on "Gone Away" are as enjoyable as their album versions. The tight performances, coupled with Butch Vig's masterful engineering, make tracks like "Man in the Trees" hit considerably harder, while some of the *Century Days* tracks feel eerily close to the album versions.

Keith: We got a lot of blowback because people really doubted that those were live recordings. A lot of people commented on that.

Erik: We were well rehearsed. We knew how to play those songs, and that's why they ended up sounding the way they did.

Butch Vig: They were so good as a band, and ultimately that's why it ended up sounding as good as it does.

The Hard Report wrote, "'Gone Away' sways like a dead tree in the wind, whose branches are hanging on for dear life when a strong gust hits. ... I've not heard a more compelling song this year." *CMJ* wrote, "['Gone Away'] is a song as good as any they've ever done, a creeping, hypnotic crawl of a ballad that finds Dan Kubinski's voice slowly building to its trademark disemboweling screech, while Brian Egeness—surely one of the best guitars on the indie circuit—throws glistening effect laden electric embellishments over the song's brittle acoustic textures." *Melody Maker* wrote, "Rarely has rock music been so feverishly melodic. The electric guitar ceaselessly baits and blisters the melancholic shiver of the gingerly picked acoustic and, with both tracks, Dan Kubinski's rugged voice first scrambles, then roars and finally soars above the struggle."

NME praised the song for its unconventionality, writing, "In much the same manner as Joy Division's celestial drones followed on from punk, 'Gone Away' relocates metal styles in a minefield of experimentation. ... People will try and tell you there's something valid in hardcore's caterwauling urban sprawl. I say start all over again. The only worthwhile acts are the ones who've done something with the stagnant genre, starting with Die Kreuzen."

Alternative Press praised the release in its entirety, noting that, "While scores of their contemporaries and adoring descendants have gone on to make flashes in the mainstream daylight, Die Kreuzen has remained a fixture of the independent underground. If they want a major deal, they'll surely have their pick, given the suitability of the melancholy metal they've been flirting with lately to the corporate music business's current appetite for aggressive guitar bands. This disk demonstrates that Die Kreuzen need that kind of legitimacy in order to ensure that they are acknowledged by the history books for their imprint on modern music."

Sounds named "Gone Away" its Single of the Week, saying "Gone Away, although not exactly mind-exploding, is a surprise and a treat. Above all, it runs on pure passion—which is, as always, what wins the day every time."

Running on passion was very much the modus operandi with Die Kreuzen. Though the band had still not made the jump from Touch and Go to a major label, the majors were once again starting to take notice of the underground. The hopes they had for the Replacements and Hüsker Dü didn't fully pan out, but other acts like REM, the Cure, and Depeche Mode had fully broken into the mainstream by this point. Even seemingly less-commercial thrash metal acts like Metallica and Slayer proved that MTV and radio airplay weren't entirely needed to play larger venues and enjoy respectable record sales.

Corey Rusk: You could feel that something was happening in that we were selling more and more records. It wasn't just us; independent labels in general were selling more records, which only meant that more people from the mainstream were starting to become interested in it. There was starting to be coverage of independent records in more mainstream magazines than there had ever been up to that point. Something was definitely happening. At the time, I don't know if I could have predicted or told you what it was, but there was a growing swell of interest in bands on indie record labels.

Die Kreuzen's peerless sonic identity allowed them to continually grow as an underground act in the latter half of the decade. Throughout their career, the band was consistently on the radar of one or more labels, as A&R execs certainly took note of both the critical acclaim the band was receiving and their dedicated fanbase. Having their pick of major label offers wasn't quite the case, but in 1989 MCA Records began talking to the band about signing with Mechanic Records. Mechanic was an imprint

they created for more aggressively-minded acts, with a roster that featured Dream Theater as well as Voivod, the French-Canadian progressive metal band who often drew comparisons to Die Kreuzen. The interest from Mechanic certainly made more sense than Profile, so the band began to talk with the label to see what they could offer them.

Keith: I can't really recall how the MCA/Mechanic situation exactly came about. I just remember we were in New York and ended up taking a meeting with them because they were interested in our band.

Butch Vig: They called and explained that MCA/Mechanic was interested in signing Die Kreuzen and that they wanted them to record some demos for the label. They wanted me to come up with a budget and time frame, and I thought that it would be great to have a month at Smart to work on the songs. To me, that was a luxury.

Keith: We went to the Mechanic offices. Steve Sinclair was our contact there, and he was pretty much like, "Here's some money, make some demos!" We'd go to Smart and record some demos and he'd just be like, "Eh, I dunno—make some more!" and gave us more money for demos.

Butch Vig: The band wanted to do the demos and make their next record with me at Smart, but the label had their own suggestions for studios and engineers.

Keith: We ended up getting a couple thousand dollars just to do demos. I don't know if they were just burning money for tax write-offs or whatever.

Butch Vig: Steve Sinclair called me at Smart one day. I remember him having this sort of Long Island accent, just saying to me, "I don't know who you ahh." He was kind of blunt, but rightfully so. He didn't have any confidence in my abilities because I think from his point of view it was just like, "Who's this guy from Wisconsin working at this punk rock studio? What has he done?" or whatever.

Keith: Except, you know, produce a bunch of records on Touch and Go that sold a ton [laughs].

Butch Vig: He pretty much told me point blank that I wasn't ready to do a major-label record. I had just finished working on [the Smashing Pumpkins debut album] *Gish*, but I don't think it had been released yet. It's funny to think about that now.

Die Kreuzen visit the Berlin wall, c. 1989. Photo courtesy of Die Kreuzen. Photographer unknown.

Brian: I remember they were talking about having us get some guy to produce an album for, like, $35,000. I remember us thinking that if we had Butch do the record, we could've used that money for not only our recording but also videos and promotion or whatever.

By this point in their career, signing to a major label felt like the next logical step the band should take. For a band who placed artistry and creativity ahead of commerciality, though, the process of entertaining offers proved to be frustrating. Making music with a limited budget could only do so much, but the band made the most with the limited resources they had, putting out records that looked and sounded great. Signing with a major surely made sense but, after three situations with three different major labels never materializing, the concept began to feel less and less appealing to the band.

Keith: I was starting to get really disillusioned with that whole brass-ring thing. Did we really want to be on a label like Mechanic? I remember being pretty direct about trying to see what they wanted to do, but at the same time we really were only going to sign with a label if they gave us the things that we wanted—creative control and all that. I wasn't remarkably bothered, I guess. I wished that Touch and Go had better distribution, but the amount of money it would take for them to get their records in a place like Best Buy or whatever, it would just be so disproportionate in relation to the number of records that would actually sell. We were somehow convinced that if we could just get our records into places like Kmart, that they would actually sell.

Erik: On top of all that, Mechanic's parent company contacted us directly as well. I think they were trying to undermine whatever that we had going with Mechanic. Suddenly, we were stuck in between some kind of situation with a label and their parent company. Just classic major-label politics.

Keith: Regardless of what we may have been told or believed, the concept of us having any kind of control over anything we did, be it recording or song choices or album art, that stuff would have eventually been under the discretion of the people in charge.

Butch Vig: Had they signed to Mechanic, there's a really high chance that it would have ended badly. They probably would have made a great-sounding record that the label had no idea what to do with, put a single out, and then go on tour and do a pretty good tour but not expand beyond what they were doing already. By the time the prospect of the second record would come around, it would've been a huge question mark as to whether the label would get behind them again or just drop them, because that happened *all* the time.

Die Kreuzen were well rehearsed and finishing tracking demos with plenty of time left over. Had it been their own budget at stake, recording would have ended, but since the sessions were already paid for, the band used the remaining studio time to record a single for Touch and Go. Instead of recording new songs, though, the band decided to pay homage to some of their earliest influences.

Keith: We finished the demos and had some time left over, and we wanted to use it up, so we just decided to do some songs. We ended up doing the cover seven-inch with that budget. A lot of bands released a bunch of singles in a year, but they'd often not be that great, just like a bunch of throwaway songs. I felt like if we were going to put out a single, it would have to have something interesting on it. The rationale behind it was that the single would come out significantly before the album, so it would almost be, like, a way of promoting the album. We'd send those out to radio, and that would be a way of letting people know that a full-length was in the works.

Dan: We used to do a couple of Germs covers going as far back as the Stellas.

Keith: They were both bands we listened to a lot early on. I remember playing that Germs record incessantly and I had been listening to Wire since I was in high school. We still listened to both of those records and loved them. We'd sometimes pull out "Pink Flag" as an encore in the live shows, which was great 'cause you could go out there and just kinda wing it.

Keith: We were tracking "Pink Flag" and did a whole bunch of takes, and for whatever reason Erik couldn't get the ending right. I was starting to lose patience with him, and I remember saying something to him over the talkback, and I'm pretty sure he was ready to kill me, and he just took his sticks and threw them on the ground, right at the end of this take. We didn't really have every single take to choose from like you could have today. We had to reuse the two-inch tape that we had previously recorded on.

If you play it, you can hear the sticks fall and then all of a sudden the music comes back in really loud—that's actually the end of an earlier take that just happened to come in after this one ended. Just completely by chance, completely out of the blue. We were playing the take back and we hear this happen and we're just elated: "*That's it! That's the ending!*" We're all freaking out and Butch was just so confused.

Butch Vig: I remember that we had to record over previous takes of the song, because two-inch tape was too expensive to keep multiple reels with different takes on them. Because we were recording over things, sometimes a previous take was audible even though it was erased!

Keith: It was just the most amazing surreal coincidence that could have happened. It's totally unrepeatable—there's no way we could've recreated that. That was pretty insane and, honestly, if you're working digitally, those kinds of happy accidents just don't happen.

Each side of "Pink Flag" / "Land of Treason" represents an element of Die Kreuzen's sound. "Pink Flag" highlights the patient and artful side of the band, while "Land of Treason" is an exercise in straightforward aggression. Intentional or not, the single release showed listeners that the band hadn't strayed from their roots. All of their early influences were still present; it just wasn't always as easy to spot them.

"Land of Treason" is the most straightforward of the two, with the band pummeling through the classic Germs track in a similar fashion to the original. The band frantically tears through the track with life and vibrance while Kubinski chooses to sing the song an octave higher than how it originally appears. The track sounds, quite literally, like what one would expect Die Kreuzen covering the Germs in 1989 to sound like.

Corey Rusk: It was totally a no-brainer. I thought they were great cover versions, and I thought it was a cool contrast to what they were doing. It wasn't like they just wrote a couple hardcore songs and put out a hardcore single; they picked these classic punk songs and did them in a very Die Kreuzen sort of way. I remember hearing that and thinking, "How amazing are they?"

"Pink Flag," the title track from Wire's 1977 debut LP, is, at its core, a relatively simple song. Die Kreuzen's take on it is a bit more complex than their version of "Land of Treason." The driving two-chord trudge is bolstered by Vig's bombastic production, amplifying the song's melodicism and giving it an anthemic quality. As the song picks up speed it eventually begins to fall off the rails. Ultimately, Tunison and Brammer's rhythmic foundation crumbles, Kubinski's vocals squeal like tires before a collision, and Egeness's guitars engulf it all like flames.

Kohl's scorched-car imagery for the single visually complements the ending of "Pink Flag" specifically. The dual-sided sleeve presented two sides of his own artistic style—one more minimal and angular, the other side featuring layers of blown-out xerox imagery and splashes of fluorescent colors.

Richard Kohl: I put a lot of thought into all this stuff—it was a lot of fun. A lot of it is loaded imagery. If you load it up a bit more, it just becomes more interesting. People try to make a connection between the images, and sometimes there's a connection there and sometimes there's not.

Writers praised the single and the band's fresh take on the two covers. Rockpool [a newsletter for radio DJs active during the eighties and nineties] notes that "'Pink Flag' is about the only song on *Pink Flag* that we haven't heard covered a zillion times, but Die K add their metallic edge and an almost (early) Pink Floyd-like love of corrosive clutter that makes this stand out, ...The Germs' cover is even more manic than the late Darby Crash and mates' version, and Crash's unsettled snarl is replaced with the trademark high-pitched screeching vocals that graces all their records. Easily a shining moment for this band who continues to grow and shine."

CMJ wrote, "Die Kreuzen bow down to a couple of universal punk influences (Wire and the Germs), though they could've been just as historically relevant if they'd chosen to cover their own 'On the Street' or 'Hate Me' from that first LP. ...Windmills with arms of righteous flame saw through both covers, monolith guitars filling every available cranny in the mix with onrushing volume. The fact that Die Kreuzen is able to add some bombast and Odin's wrath to songs by notoriously concise, straightforward bands just goes to show that they can out rock-star any Headbanger's Ball pet."

In six years, Die Kreuzen had gone from being one of hardcore punk's most revered newcomers to something more expansive, dynamic, and forward-thinking. As the new decade began, their critical acclaim continued to increase, and many of their peers started to see success beyond the underground. Independently of this, the band continued to move forward, following their own agenda on their own terms. ●

The always-evolving look of Die Kreuzen c. 1990.
Photo: Marty Graham

Cement and the End of Die Kreuzen

BY 1991, THE STYLE AND SOUND OF MAINSTREAM GUITAR rock had shifted considerably and, with that, so had the archetype of the kind of band that could enjoy mainstream success. Sonic Youth recently released their major-label debut Goo on DGC, as had Soundgarden the year prior. Jane's Addiction had their mainstream breakthrough in 1990 with *Ritual de lo Habitual*. Although they were still technically on the independent label Mute, Depeche Mode achieved massive success with their *Violator* album. The boundaries of mainstream rock bands had shifted far enough to where Die Kreuzen had a chance of finally breaking through, but they were still trying to find their place in the music world—too heavy for REM fans and too melodic for the hardcore crowd. They often were ahead of their contemporaries, but for the first time in their career the tastes of the mainstream were beginning to catch up to them.

The joy of creation continued to fuel the writing and recording of their next album. Regardless of the changing landscape of the mainstream, the band wrote the same way they always had, putting self-satisfaction first. The busy touring schedule coupled with their already slow writing process resulted in a longer writing period for their next album. The band always strove to give the songs their full attention and ample time to be fully developed before committing them to tape.

Keith: When we would typically write, either myself or Dan would come in with pretty much fully formed ideas. We used to go in and just pick the good bits from the bad bits, but as time went on, it was easier to just have a solid idea and be like, "Okay, here's how this goes."

It was easier for me to have a bassline and super-rudimentary guitars. Brian would come in with these more complex kinds of parts that were based around one chord, so it didn't leave much room for bass. Both of us had these fully formed ideas, and we'd be completely intractable about them.

Dan: I don't think there was any purposeful or conscious effort on anyone's part to write something that was more commercial or had hit potential. It was just the next batch of songs. Some of those songs even go back to around the time of *Century Days*.

Keith: It got to where both Brian and I were coming in with things, but we didn't always want to do the same things, so that sometimes caused some conflict. It got to be, like, how things get—you just go your separate ways. I think we made it work well because it doesn't sound like that; it doesn't sound fragmented. If you were someone who knew our individual styles, though, you could kind of tell on *Cement* whose songs were whose.

Brian: We still put 100% of ourselves into the writing and recording of the material.

Erik: At the time we were working hard at it, we weren't phoning it in at all.

In early 1991, the band made their second appearance on Milwaukee public-access television. Performing amongst dense layers of fog, surrounded by chain-link fencing, the band rips through seven new songs. The look and sound are undoubtedly Die Kreuzen and, sonically, the band sounds as tight as ever. There's a confidence and intensity on display here with the band's performance that make it feel as though they're performing at a packed club. Reviewing live footage at the time reveals little difference between this performance and their actual live gigs.

Initial demos of new material were recorded with Steve Albini in his Chicago home studio. These were quick sessions but, despite the quick turnaround, the recordings stand on their own as great documents of the songs.

Steve Albini: For a while there, I was running a studio out of the basement of my house. It was a super-cheap recording option, so if bands needed to do a track for a compilation or they needed a B side for a single, I ended up doing a lot of those. One-off odd collaborations and projects and such.

I have to admit, I kind of lost interest later, as their music became more elaborate and more involved, and probably could have been kinder towards them personally.

Had they chosen to do the entire album with Albini, the album would've been perfectly enjoyable. Based on their strong working relationship, however, the band chose to once again work with Butch Vig.

By this point, Vig's reputation was starting to spread. Due in part to his work on Killdozer's 1989 album *Twelve Point Buck*, Vig was quickly becoming an in-demand producer for artists from the Midwest and beyond. Not long after Vig wrapped up work on the Smashing Pumpkins' debut album *Gish*, in the summer of 1991, Die Kreuzen returned to Smart Studios to record their final album, *Cement*. The band had a longer stretch of time to work on the album but, despite this added luxury, the sessions weren't nearly as much of a group effort as their previous sessions had been.

Butch Vig: I really liked the songs that they were writing around the time we started work on that record.

Keith: That record was hard to make, harder than anything we had done. It was generally frustrating for me at least, and I started drinking more because of that.

The *Cement* sessions were the only time when I wasn't there for the entire session. I came in and did my parts with Erik, and then I went back to Milwaukee to go back to work. I couldn't spend an infinite amount of time there.

Erik: It doesn't necessarily help to have the drummer sit there like a vulture while the singer is trying to bare his soul on the microphone.

Butch Vig: The *Cement* sessions were really smooth. I had a good rapport with the band at that point. In terms of their performances, they were firing on all cylinders. They had been playing together for so long that they had this sixth sense in terms of the dynamic between them. That's not to say that there wouldn't be disagreements on how parts or arrangements were supposed to be, but that's also just a part of the creative process.

Dan: I think we went in on a Friday and Erik and Keith worked that whole weekend, getting all the rhythm tracks done. Both went home because they had to work. Brian and I stayed at a friend's house that was walking distance from the studio, and I think we had another week left for us to work on getting everything else done.

The plan was to do the guitars for a day or two and spend the rest of the time doing vocals and mixing. From my recollection, I remember Brian kept doing parts repeatedly. He just kept thinking that he could do better than the last one. He'd be changing parts from take to take. I think he had a lot of different ideas in his head, but to me it felt like he was trying to fit a bunch of stuff into the spaces.

Brian: I remember changing things because I wasn't happy with what I was playing. We had more time and a budget, and I wanted to take advantage of that.

Butch Vig: The music was becoming more diverse and complex-sounding, and I encouraged that. By then, every song didn't have to be fast; they had so much talent and so many ideas that, for me, I just wanted to be able to harness those ideas and make sure that they still sounded like Die Kreuzen.

I worked Dan hard on that record in terms of his singing, and we spent a lot more time on the vocals for that record than we did for *Century Days*. The songs on *Cement* were much more melody-driven than those on their previous records, so I wanted to get the best performances out of Dan. The way I mixed him there, too, was different from their previous records. I didn't want to bury his voice or make it too affected like it had been in the past. I think I just wanted the album to over all sound really crisp and in your face.

Dan: I think we might have ended up going over the time we had booked and had to book more time in the end.

Erik: I remember working day and night on mixes, and then the next day having Butch come in early and he'd show us some mixes he did on his own that were much better than whatever we had in mind. We probably should have learned earlier to keep the four band members away from the desk and let the producer do his job. Especially with Butch being a supremely talented and experienced guy, we should have done that.

Keith: The upshot was that he ended up mixing most of that without our assistance. If anybody was being obstreperous, Butch could talk to people without feeling like they were being yelled at. He was great at that.

Richard Kohl handled the album's art direction once again. From the beginning, Die Kreuzen fans were treated to a broad palate of visuals created by Kohl, from the ominous black-and-white photography of *October File* to the layered xerox-manipulated imagery on *Century Days*. For *Cement*, Kohl returned to the minimalism of just pen and ink. The result was hardly something nostalgic or self-referential, though. *Cement*'s album art remains just as timeless and progressive as anything else in their discography, with Kohl once again finding an opportunity to manipulate text to suit his specific visual aesthetic.

Richard: For the *Cement* cover, I went back to pen-and-ink drawing. That one is probably my favorite of all the covers. I love them all, but that one to me is my favorite. All the type, I did those things purposefully. If I recall, I probably did those on a typewriter and blew them up. When you blow up type, it shows all of the minor imperfections, which I love.

The album sleeve once again features no lyrics but does include an extensive thank-you list, with each member getting their own section. Egeness keeps it short and sweet, thanking his friends and family and fans for the support. Tunison uses the opportunity to speak on his wishes for a less violent world, criticizing its glorification in films and on TV. Kubinski and Brammer speak on the band's now-decade-long career with gratitude, honesty, and sincerity.

Brammer's contribution reads as follows: "ten years, times are it seems like it, and times are it seems impossible? loads of adventures (good and bad), but no regrets here. we did it our way, to coin a phrase. books have been made of (much) less and one day ... who knows?"

How prophetic.

Thank-you lists often feel like a place to give respect to those to whom it is due. *Cement*'s liner notes read a bit more reflective, expressing uncertainty of the future. Both Brammer and Kubinski specifically point out the struggles the band endured, but still the band maintains that at the time of the album there were no immediate plans of dissolving the band.

Butch Vig: I could tell there was a little bit of internal conflict with the band by then, but that happens with all bands. It didn't feel like they were making their last record or that they were going to break up. I don't know if the band members felt it or not, but if they did it certainly didn't show in their attitudes or their work on that album.

Is *Cement* Die Kreuzen's pop record? Not exactly. The evolution toward more melodic songwriting was organic, and ultimately the songs were still written by the same group of people who had written "Enemies" nearly a decade before. *Cement* is a more patient and mid-paced record, but those who spend time with it will eventually be able to hear elements of the band's earlier material on it, albeit delivered in a different way. The spirit of the band's early work exists as an enhancement, using intensity and dissonance as spices to season otherwise melodic songs.

Every Die Kreuzen album is its own individual color in the larger picture of the band's catalog and, regardless of how the music evolved, it always sounded like Die Kreuzen. Where *Century Days* still maintained some of the blurry haze of the band's previous two albums, *Cement*'s production is one of its defining characteristics. *Cement* was their first full-length produced at Vig's home base Smart Studios, and his extreme familiarity with both the room and the equipment allowed him to provide the band with the best possible outcome. Building on the melodic foundation laid by "Gone Away," Kubinski's vocals are mixed slightly higher than usual, making his lyrics more discernible than on any of their previous albums.

Cement is the most straightforward rock-sounding record in their discography. Shades of '70s rock shine brighter, especially in the guitar playing and vocal performances. One could also make the argument that those influences were always there and that they are simply more at the forefront in this batch of songs.

October File sounded like a forerunner for post-hardcore in the mid-'80s. *Cement* does the same but for the early '90s, drawing from a similar well as East Coast acts who used heavy guitars to craft melody-focused songs and a more emotional vocal delivery. But, like *Century Days* before it, *Cement* has its moments of shrieking terror as well.

The release of "Gone Away," whether conscious or not, proved to be an apt preview for where the band was moving. Many of the tracks on *Cement* employ the song's rolling 6/8 groove and somber mood and lean towards more melodic songwriting.

The album opens with a wash of droning guitars before quickly kicking into "Wish," a midtempo track that feels familiar and fresh all at once. The chord progression alone gives this song an emotional weight reminiscent of "Gone Away." That song stays in one lane, though, while "Wish" takes it elsewhere, at times sounding like several songs in one. It's busier than most Die Kreuzen songs in its arrangement, and it's one of the first songs to feature a fade-out ending. Still, it manages to not lose the listener entirely, and Egeness's guitar solo, while more traditional than his usual fare, still sounds unmistakably like him.

Beginning with minimal, wandering solo guitars that eventually give way to the entire band, "Shine" feels like a twisted take on early Aerosmith, with Egeness taking a hypnotic and dizzying guitar solo towards the song's latter half. "Shine" was performed live as early as 1988, making it one of the album's older tracks. Though it would probably have fit better on the second half of *Century Days* than the first half of *Cement*, it's one of the album's more aggressive tracks, driven by Kubinski's puncturing screams.

This isn't to say that the album feels undercooked, as *Cement* has plenty of moments that possess a swagger and self-assuredness that can only come from years of writing, recording, and touring.

"Big Bad Days," which saw its own single release, is one of the album's brightest moments. It takes nearly thirty seconds for the song to take off, starting with the sound of Egeness's distant guitars, but when the track finally arrives the listener is treated to the closest thing the album has to an outright pop song. Both the verses and choruses are melodically strong, and the bass and drums tether it to the ground, giving room for Egeness and Kubniski to weave in and out of the arrangements. There's a massive, soaring quality about "Big Bad Days" that feels very much like a group effort; all four members carry the song to make it work.

"Holes" serves as an apt reminder of the band's status as a Touch and Go act, with its chunky bass-and-drum groove and mid-song false stop. Kubinski, Brammer, and Tunison's performances all give the song the distinct Die Kreuzen touch. Meanwhile, Egeness's riffs and use of dissonance still recall his singular playing style, but on "Holes" and throughout the entirety of *Cement* Egeness uses his guitar's whammy bar more than ever. Still, his technique was quite different from what was commonly heard on rock records at the time, with guitar players usually using it as a means of intensifying virtuosic guitar solos. Egeness's approach is more abstract,

The *Cement* album cover featuring Richard Kohl's complex visual geometry. Kohl put as much work into his album art as the band did into the music.

instead using the tool to warp and smear notes, creating tones and textures that don't immediately register as guitar. It's a progressive approach to the instrument that's done with taste, woven into his overall playing style. The result is an approach that can only be described as a strange hybrid of Jimi Hendrix and Kevin Shields.

"Downtime" shows Kubinski covering new ground in his vocal performance, featuring layered tracks of Kubinski harmonizing with multiple tracks of himself. Kubinski had employed this practice on the band's cover of "Pink Flag" just a year or so prior, and on "Downtime" he uses it to fine effect, layering close harmonies that give the song an audibly wide stereo image.

"Deep Space" feels like it's coming from the same place as "Cool Breeze" from *October File*, more understated and somber than many of the album's other tracks, with the band laying down a comfortable REM-esque jangle. The smooth and airy bass flute of John Kruth presents a sound and texture the band had yet to explore, and the inclusion of new instrumentation shows that the band was continuing to expand their sonic vocabulary.

As a bonus track, the band includes an acoustic version of "Gone Away." Most of *Cement* feels like the direct descendent of "Gone Away," so its inclusion on the album makes sense. Including an alternate version of the track shows it in a different light, stripping away the aggressive elements of the song and leaving the listener with the song's melodic and emotional core. Kubinski sings in a far more reserved manner, accompanied by Brammer, Tunison, Egeness, and Kruth on mandolin, all matching his laid-back delivery. The band played a few acoustic gigs around this time, and even spoke of discussing considering a more acoustic-focused album, though nothing ever materialized beyond a loose plan.

The influence of '70s rock juxtaposed with a post-punk and hardcore influence alluded to a sound that eventually dominated the mainstream. Additionally, the album's more melancholic qualities—like Brammer's basslines on tracks like "Blue Song" and "Heaven"—just barely predate acts like Sunny Day Real Estate and Texas Is the Reason, acts whose music had a similar emotive low-end foundation. Hearing the album now, *Cement* sounds like a band who were in a state of transition. They cover a vast amount of territory, and as a result the album sounds like a band trying to figure out where they want to go next. Die Kreuzen were an act who kept evolving, and every album felt like a new chapter in the story. *Cement* is an interesting step forward and an enjoyable record in its own

right, but in many ways it feels like a smaller step leading up to a much bigger leap.

Kim Thayil: *Cement* to me was just fantastic. There's things on *Cement* that still fucking grab me. That's where Dan really starts working with harmonies, and it really opened up my perception of what I thought Die Kreuzen was. No one's making you do the same thing, right? You're gonna grow and change and incorporate new elements into how you write and what you play. The guitar playing was great; the arrangements were great. There was something really cool about Butch's production perspective. It was new—it was like adding these elements to whatever you already liked about Die Kreuzen.

Jon Wurster: I just remember hearing "Deep Space" and hearing the most gorgeous bass flute solo and thinking, "This is what I love about this band—they have a bass flute solo on a record on Touch and Go Records in 1991" [laughs]. I can't say enough about that aspect of Die Kreuzen: they were always so willing to try something new, and it almost always worked. They worked so well with Butch, and I think he understood them so well, so their records always sounded really great.

Corey Rusk: I definitely pushed that record a little bit harder because of where I knew they wanted to be, but also because I knew where I wanted them to be. I believed in them all the way until the end, and I thought *Cement* was a great record. It was that time where things were slowly starting to change, and maybe I thought that their time had finally come. Maybe this will be the one, because all along I kept feeling like there should be a wider audience for them, and when it wouldn't happen, then the next record was the next opportunity to try and make it happen.

Among the reviews of *Cement* was a feature from the July 1992 issue of *Hit Parader* titled "The 20 Bands Most Likely to Shake the Rock World,", with Die Kreuzen appearing on the same page as the Afghan Whigs and the Smashing Pumpkins. Die Kreuzen's blurb reads short but sweet: "Of all the bands currently in the metal underground, Die Kreuzen has the most potential to make it in mainstream rock music." Quite an impressive statement, but somehow the major-label system didn't see it the same way. Profile Records aside, Die Kreuzen were never formally offered a deal with any major label, despite getting close with Elektra and MCA/Mechanic. By the time *Cement* was out, the band had started to wonder if they even wanted to take that path.

Brian: It would've been nice. We were just getting tired of doing the same thing on every tour and playing to the same people. We loved Touch and Go, but I think, like a lot of bands that were signing to majors at the time, we were just looking for a level of support that Touch and Go couldn't offer us at that time, especially in relation to distribution. They were fantastic—they were doing the absolute most that they could've done for us at that time.

Butch Vig: The fact that they weren't easy to define was great for them musically. In terms of a career, it can be tricky. Major labels and the mainstream like to be able to pigeonhole a band, because then you can get slotted into whatever MTV or FM-radio playlist. Even college radio back then was sometimes just as discriminatory as top-forty radio. It really all depended on whether you fit into whatever kinda vibe the station was trying to push at the time. If you fell into a category that was easily understood, it was easier to get more airplay and reach a bigger audience. The bands who didn't do that, it made it tougher on them, but those were often the best bands.

Corey Rusk: I always felt that for the most part, the bands on the label, including Die Kreuzen, what they were doing was far enough left of center that the chances of real mainstream success . . . if it was going to happen, if it was in the cards for the bands, we could make it happen, and that a major label wasn't necessarily going to understand them properly enough to make it happen. That was my view, but at the same time I wasn't the sort of person who was going to totally try and guilt a band into staying on the label. The bands that I work with were my friends. Die Kreuzen are my friends. If they all felt that they had to sign with a major, I wasn't going to try and talk them out of it. Any discussion at that time, if they were talking about the possibility . . . I always encouraged bands that I worked with to just be honest with me. If you're talking to majors or whatever, I just wanted them to be honest.

Keith: They'd [major labels] just sign a ton of bands and just throw them all at the wall to see what sticks. For as much as we wanted to be on a bigger label, the more I think about it, it really would have killed our band stone dead. We probably would've ended up owing tons and tons of money to some label.

Corey Rusk: Over the years, if you look at any of the bands from Touch and Go that ended up going to majors—like Urge Overkill, the Jesus Lizard,

Girls Against Boys—if you look at the records that they made while on a major label, none of them became that next big thing. I loved all those bands, and the records they made for Touch and Go were amazing.

If you look at sales figures for bands who made the jump from an indie label to a major label, a lot of them didn't sell much more on a major than they would have had they released that same record on the same indie label that they had been working with for years. Some of them maybe sold a few more records, but was it enough to make the major label happy or significantly increase the public's awareness of them? From my perspective, it didn't appear that that was the case.

Keith: It's really about who you know or who one of your friends knows. It had less to do with whether you had a huge fanbase or whether you were going to sell records. It was about someone who loved your band working at the label and making a case for your band. The flip side of that, of course, is thirteen months later when your friend at the label gets fired. Then you're just shit out of luck.

Erik: I wasn't frustrated about that personally. I felt like we were so fortunate to be on Touch and Go and be able to field these sorts of offers from a position of strength. We didn't have to accept a bad offer.

Butch Vig: It's hard to speculate about it now and it would have really depended on the sort of songs they wrote, but even if they had remained where they were stylistically, I think it would have fit in well with the current scene at that time, but at the same time been different, so they would have stood apart from some of their contemporaries and had their own identity.

Still, the band had a new album to promote and did a fair amount of touring in support of it, playing shows in the South, on the East Coast, and for a few dates out west.

Keith: At that point we weren't touring quite as much. We all had different jobs and different lives outside of the band.

Dan: After *Cement* came out, we went out on tour and on so many shows there'd still be four or five of these fast-paced hardcore bands opening up for us, one after the other. I remember every night showing up at the venue and seeing all the kids running around with mohawks and shit. It just became a joke.

Richard Kohl: I saw that element. It's tragic. This stuff just boils down to where you get to this point and it's just the lumpenproletariat being awful. They're all still around—they look exactly the same and have the same fucking bad attitude. They have their dogs with them and it's just ... ugh it's the fucking worst.

Keith: We used to have it in the contract that we didn't want to play with hardcore bands, but everyone just ignored that.

Dan: Just a few years prior, we had been in Europe on tour with Sonic Youth and the Laughing Hyenas., and that was a real kick in the ass for us. We'd be playing to audiences of like a thousand-plus people, but then we came back to the States and we'd be back to playing to the same two hundred people in every city. We just weren't getting to that next level.

Keith: I know it sounds ungrateful, because now two hundred people at a show is a great turnout, but it was just a different time. We started growing apart musically, as cliché as that sounds. We never phoned it in when it came to the live shows. We were always putting 100% in because people paid to see us. That was our attitude. Even if there were six people in the audience, those six people paid to see you. If you put on a shitty show because there weren't enough people there, the people who were there would probably tell their friends, and then no one would come see you the next time you came through town. I know that because I've seen shows like that where a band just doesn't care, and it made me reconsider going to see them again.

From day one, growth and creativity were the main concern for the band. The band's music continued to evolve, but by the time *Cement* was released things started to feel like they were slowing down. Up to this point, there had always been noticeable benchmarks met—recording a demo, touring, putting out an album, leaving the states, etc. By 1992, the band had virtually done it all, but breaking into the upper echelon proved to be challenging. Intra-band conflicts began to rise and more.

Brian: I think by that point we just lost our purpose. I think we were confused as to what we wanted to do. There was frustration as to where we were as a band.

Keith: Everybody had an idea of what we should be doing that was kind of different from each other.

Erik: It was no longer us on this upward trajectory. We were clearly seeing that.

Keith: It started gradually around the time of the second European tour. For a good few years there, we were just on tour constantly, and it really started to cause issues. When we were at home, things were okay. We had just got to a certain point, just moving up the ladder, but eventually it felt like it had stagnated.

Brian: After so many years, we just wanted to move to that next level because we were constantly wanting to move forward. That desire to move forward didn't affect the material or how we wrote songs, but it affected our band on a business level.

Dan: We really worked hard to get to the point where we were, and it seemed like everyone else was getting to that next level except for us.

Brian: We just wanted to be able to do it full-time. I was tired of working at fuckin' pizzerias.

Keith: Drinking was outside the sphere of the band and, back then, everyone drank. It was the culture we were in—you'd get booze when you got to the show or whatever. There were a couple of shows where I kind of took it too far and realized it once I got on stage, and even then I would just have to soldier through it. I worked hard to ensure that that didn't happen.

Everyone had their own individual issues, and we were far from perfect people. I'm just stating a fact—I had a bad drinking problem. I don't think it affected the band unduly, but at the same time it couldn't help but have some sort of impact. As embarrassing as that was, I don't think it affected us playing or writing, but it affected the way I was living.

People started to lose it a little bit, and it just became uncomfortable to function as a band. It just got to the point where everything just became very difficult. We just weren't really getting along that well. I was losing my patience with having to constantly argue about things. Communication started to become different.

Steve Albini: When you start a band, you have this rush of ideas that you come up with, like that first album has twenty-plus songs on it. There's an initial rush of creativity, and riding that rush is really exciting; you're going downhill, and everything is picking up momentum all the time, faster and faster and greater and greater. Then you hit the bottom of the hill, and you still have some momentum from that initial rush, but you're also kind of coasting on that for a bit. You have to exert yourself to keep up to speed, and as that energy and initial enthusiasm dies out, then it's *all* on you. You have to do all of the pedaling to keep the band going in any meaningful way.

After doing it for a few years, people remember how easy it used to be, and when you have to come up with new ideas all the time your ideas start to wear thin. I don't think there was anything about their changing style that indicated a decline. Those first couple of years and records made an indelible impression, and after that they were running the band to suit themselves. They were trying just as hard—it's just not as easy to keep things going after so many years. It's just a much more difficult enterprise

Keith: You can't expect four guys to basically live in each other's pockets for ten years and expect for there to not be any conflict. We didn't have the luxury of a bus or separate hotel rooms—it was, "Get in the van and let's drive for twelve hours and then we can all share a Motel 6 if we're lucky."

Brian: I think we were halfway home, and I told them that I was gonna leave after the tour was over.

Keith: At the end, I was tired and frustrated. When Brian said that, I let out a sigh of relief.

Erik: It was Brian who quit but I also didn't have any problem with it. Seemed like a good idea—I can agree. It had been twelve years and we're not really moving any further. I believe it was Nick Mason from Pink Floyd who said, "It got so bad, we nearly said something." Somebody finally spoke up and said something. It just happened to be Brian who said it first.

On April 1, 1992, Dan Kubinski, Brian Egeness, Erik Tunison, and Keith Brammer performed as Die Kreuzen for the last time at the University of Wisconsin-Milwaukee Ballroom.

Keith: Brian decided to leave, and our last show ended up being our show at UWM. We decided to play the show and not say anything about it until after. At that point, we weren't really playing in Milwaukee all that much—maybe once a month? We just decided it was the last show, and after the fact so many people were like, "You should have told us," and we were just like, "Well, you should've been there."

Corey Rusk: I was somewhat aware that there had been some tensions within the band, so I guess it wasn't a total surprise.

Above: Die Kreuzen perform live at the Metroplex in Atlanta, Georgia, in 1991. Photo: Ken Kelly.

Below: Die Kreuzen performing live for the last time at the UWM Ballroom in Milwaukee, April 1992. Photo courtesy of Die Kreuzen.

Jon Wurster: They were several years ahead of everyone else for much of their career. The fact that they decided to start winding down right as everyone else was starting to wind up and doing so by following a blueprint that they had partly helped write, it's a shame.

In their twelve years of existence, the band released four full-length albums and four EPs and played well over five hundred shows across America and Europe. What seemed to some like an overnight changing of the guard was actually the result of so many bands like Die Kreuzen writing, recording, and touring year after year. Not long after working on *Cement*, Butch Vig flew to Los Angeles to make Nirvana's sophomore album, *Nevermind*, one of the key albums in alternative rock's long-overdue breakthrough. By early 1992, the genre was bigger than ever, and a handful of the band's contemporaries had begun to find success beyond the underground.

Butch Vig: It wasn't just one band that made the alternative rock boom of the early '90s possible; it was a group effort.

Mike Gitter: You had almost fifteen years of hardcore, you had Jane's Addiction, you had Sonic Youth, you had Lollapalooza the summer before really organizing the demographic—the world was ready for it by this point.

Butch Vig: Die Kreuzen were definitely a part of the same wave as a ton of other bands, and they all helped pave the way. They were all chipping away at people's perception of what a rock band could be.

Corey Rusk: I think in the whole second half of the '80s, every year there was a little bit more interest from the mainstream public or press in music that was more underground. There were the occasional bands that had signed to a major and experienced moderately decent success, but they weren't selling millions of records either. Each one of those bands were a piece of the puzzle. They all broadened the general public's awareness on a subconscious level to where the average listener didn't even realize that they were becoming aware of this. And then Nirvana made a brilliant album, and it just happened at the right time.

Butch Vig: The Replacements, REM, Pixies, Hüsker Dü, and Die Kreuzen—had bands like them not existed, I'm not sure if *Nevermind* would have had the kind of success that it did. They set the template.

When you look at the success that bands like Nirvana and the Smashing Pumpkins had with the kind of music they were making, at least in the mainstream, it was expanding the mainstream's idea of what rock music could be. Had Die Kreuzen stuck together and written another record, it would have been good timing on their part. Plus, they were a great live band, and that was a big part of it too.

Corey Rusk: I wasn't friends with a lot of major-label A&R people at that point, but from my outsider perspective as a guy who ran an indie label who knew other people at indie labels, it surely appeared that many of them had carte blanche to do whatever they pleased. How many indie bands got signed to majors in the two years following the release of *Nevermind*, you know? All of a sudden, a lot of labels had no clue what could be huge. All they knew was, "If that Nirvana band could be huge, there's a whole scene full of bands like them. We don't understand which ones could be huge, so just sign as many of them as you can."

Not long after the breakup, Mike Gitter—who by then had become a brand-new A&R at Atlantic Records—attempted to sign the band. The offer came too late.

Mike Gitter: You didn't have to be a genius to do A&R at that point. There were bands that had spent time cultivating fanbases that had their own sound. You didn't need to bring in co-writers; you didn't need to doctor that much. Still, you never really knew what the outcome was going to be. Sometimes you got bands like Bad Religion and Green Day, and then sometimes you got bands like Jawbox.

Ultimately, I didn't sign Die Kreuzen, because it was very clear that, by the time I was in a position to do so, they were done: it had wound down and it was over. I wanted to sign them because they were awesome and wrote songs that got close enough where it would just take a little bit of a nudge to get them into the mainstream. It was a different world then. Had it been a couple years prior, I would've definitely signed them. Voivod was doing well by that point, and to me they were just a branch removed on the metallurgical giving tree. It was conceivable that Die Kreuzen could have sold some records.

Corey Rusk: Over the years running Touch and Go, I learned that so many things are about timing, and not necessarily timing that you can plan for. I've worked with utterly brilliant bands who were making really original, great music, who I thought would do phenomenally well, who didn't, but

I've also worked with ones who did. I'd look at them and say, "Well, why did this band do so well, but this band who was equally as brilliant and wrote equally great songs didn't?" And I really think that so much of it has to do with . . . making brilliant music and releasing it at the time when the general public is interested in that sort of music. And by interested, I don't mean already interested.

Janet Billig Rich: It's really hard to say, because so many uncommercial bands got deals, right? There's something to that idea of success being about luck and timing. It's that plus so many other variables. They had some of that X factor, and there was definitely something mysterious and cool about them. There's artists who were far less commercial than them who got signed and didn't do well, and then there's ones who did.

They were at the same intersection as a lot of other bands. Some of them, like Soundgarden, were able to cross over from being just an underground band, but then you also had things like Mudhoney and Firehose who maybe got the major record deals but weren't really able to take it to that next level. Even a band like the Jesus Lizard—there's no way that that band could have broken into the mainstream; they were just too weird. I think Die Kreuzen was at the same place that a lot of those other bands were; they just didn't end up signing to a major.

If you look at a band like Jawbox, they had that major-label moment and got into more kids' bedrooms. It didn't equate to a total commercial breakthrough, but it broadened their reach for sure. I think had Die Kreuzen signed a major-label deal, at the very least, they probably would've gotten into a few more kids' bedrooms.

Steve Albini: All bands have a lifespan, and Die Kreuzen were lucky to have burned so brightly during their tenure.

Corey Rusk: I've always felt like Die Kreuzen were ahead of their time and made these brilliant records, but when they came out it wasn't what the general public was looking for in a very mainstream sort of way.

Brian: We played everything 100% all the time. It was our music, and we weren't going to go out there and fake it. We never bent or followed anyone's rules to create the music that we did.

Keith: We always made the music that we wanted to make, and I have no regrets about that at all.

Save for a very brief writeup in the *Milwaukee Journal*, little fanfare was made out of the band's decision to break up, including from the band members themselves. And that's it, really—Die Kreuzen was over. The music they made and records they released, however, were not. Over the years, people were listening and, more specifically, musicians were listening and inspired to make their own uncompromisingly creative music. ●

The Influence and Impact of Die Kreuzen

WHEN DIE KREUZEN BROKE UP IN 1992, AFTER ELEVEN years of consistent touring and recording, the members of the band felt like it had run its course. Its members went on to do a slew of other projects in the years that followed, but none of them had the same level of impact as Die Kreuzen.

The thing with being ahead of your time, though, is that people eventually catch up. Touch and Go kept the catalog in print, making the music available to whoever wished to engage with it. Though the band were no longer active, their albums ensured that their music wouldn't be forgotten, and because of this their music influenced legions of artists who preceded them.

The influence and impact of Die Kreuzen have only grown since their formation. Whether through live shows, infamous fanzine reviews, or good-old-fashioned word of mouth, Die Kreuzen's music has continued to influence musicians over the last four decades. This is a celebration of it.

Matt Sweeney: I'm not sure why it was, but there was this time in the early '90s when certain bands who were really important in the '80s stopped being talked about. The Replacements? They just weren't discussed. I think once Nirvana blew up, the focus shifted towards all the Seattle bands. Somehow, a bunch of stuff got left behind. It's funny how trends work.

Greg Anderson: Sometimes it takes the dust to settle before people can really start to understand it. If you're making music that's very progressive and challenging like they did, a lot of times people don't understand it at the time—there's always the possibility that it may connect with them later on. To me, that's a sign of a great band.

Corey Rusk: There was never anyone else who sounded like them when they were making the music they made. Later on perhaps there were people who were adopting parts of what they were doing. Every one of those records was unique even in the sea of loud and fast hardcore records from that era; there's a lot of really great ones and a lot of really horrible ones. There's plenty of bands from back then that don't have much interest these days, but Die Kreuzen are one of the ones that there's always interest in.

Butch Vig: I think their influence has had deep tentacles. There's a lot of bands who heard Die Kreuzen, and, whether it was subliminal or not, they've used the elements of their music style in their own music. A lot of bands I've known and worked with loved the music on Touch and Go and Sub Pop. I know that it had an impact because a lot of bands that were following those labels would buy anything that they'd put out. The influence of their music runs deep, probably more so than we'll ever be able to know.

Their legacy is that the sound they created was highly influential on a lot of bands that came up in the alternative generation of music. Stylistically, it was a hybrid in terms of what they brought to the music, and a lot of young bands paid attention to that. They took what Die Kreuzen did and brought that into how they were writing. They realized that you don't have to be just one thing, that you can have all these different facets to your music. I think their songwriting and their sound was groundbreaking at the time.

Lou Barlow: They all just looked so cool, man. Even to this day, I just realize that I was trying to be this junior version of Keith with my Rickenbacker bass and big hair. Like, just from a style point of view, you just looked at him and thought, "That guy's fuckin' *cool.*"

When Dinosaur Jr. toured with the Foo Fighters for the first time, Dave Grohl had this cool little stereo in a road case that he'd bring with him backstage. Before he'd go on stage, he'd take shots of whisky and blast the first Die Kreuzen record to pump him up, like, immediately before going on stage. For me it was like "wow" because it just reminded me of how important that record was to a particular slice of musicians.

Dennis Lyxzen: They are a peripheral band in the best sense of the word—their influence is so broad. A lot of bands are playing for other musicians, and those bands sometimes become really influential, but they never get that real recognition. You ask a lot of musicians about them, and they'll say, "Yeah, I have all their records," but if you ask a normal music fan they may not know much about them.

Marilyn Mee: There's so many bands who came after Die Kreuzen that really took that kinda sound into the mainstream. When they first started getting more melodic but still maintained the edge, they had this heavy, emotional, dreamy sound. Jump ahead a little bit and look at the Smashing Pumpkins, or even a little later, bands like the Deftones. Those artists made entire careers out of blending those kinds of sounds together and were celebrated for it. Die Kreuzen were doing that much earlier on, and there really wasn't anyone else doing it at the time, at least in the same way that they were.

Brad Wood: I look at Die Kreuzen as a seminal and foundational band in my world, but their lack of commercial success can be directly tied to a target audience's inability to understand things of a more difficult nature.

Butch Vig: Die Kreuzen are one of those bands that influenced a thousand other bands that went on to have huge success. I could hear it in Soundgarden. I know Billy Corgan was aware of them, and I could hear the influence in some of the Pumpkins' more sprawling psychedelic songs.

Justin Trosper: When I listen to '90s [alternative] music, a lot of it sounds like *Century Days*, just not as good [laughs]. Bands were doing things with slightly psychedelic guitars and mixing so-called punk with metal. To me, a lot of it is very much like that record.

Damian Abraham: There's a lot of privilege that comes with growing up in the city of Toronto in that we were the record hub for all of Canada. I found *Cows and Beer* in the wild, actually.

In the early 2000s there was this hardcore revival, and everyone was starting to dig deeper into early-'80s hardcore because of bootlegs and whatnot. Everyone had the starter pack records, like the Germs records and the Black Flag records and whatnot, but people started to go about two to three layers deeper. *Cows and Beer* became this godhead record where it just had this rage and intensity to it. Then it became this quest to try and track that record down.

I feel this kind of kinship with Die Kreuzen. Fucked Up was in the same position they were in. What do you do when you don't want to keep doing the same thing over and over again? You find a way to bring what you are into what you want to be doing, and I really see them as a band who were very inspirational to us in that regard.

Dennis Lyxzen: Punk and hardcore opened up the floodgates for me and really showed me that anything was possible. That's the attitude we brought into Refused, and when I listen to the Die Kreuzen records I can totally hear that approach in the music. The first seven-inch and LP were really chaotic, but then they became something completely different over the course of the next three records. There's this attitude there of, like, "With the discovery of punk and hardcore, we can do whatever we want." For a lot of bands, punk is the starting point *and* the end point, and that's concerning, because it should be the starting point as well as the entry into an entire world of possibilities. With Die Kreuzen it's like, yeah, they were a hardcore punk band, but that didn't really define the music they played. Those barriers didn't apply to them.

There's parts of Die Kreuzen that's sort of undefined in a way, but that's also the sign of people who love music and someone who is willing to take chances out of a love for music. They were just very open-minded about music, where they wanted to go and allowing the music to take them there. The fact that they took that path and went on that journey, as a musician, I just find it really awesome and inspiring. You can tell that this really wasn't some run-of-the-mill band. Their records are challenging in all the right ways. You have to sit down and get into it—they don't play well as background music. I love those kinds of records that you have to sit down and listen to. They're great records in the sense that they're just great art.

Neko Case: I've never been less interested in them than I was when I first encountered their music. It has retained my attention this whole time. They're a seminal band for me and they're on my list of things that just make me excited about music. I've never lost my appreciation for them, and I think the whole concept of not giving a fuck about what was going around them is what has preserved them for all these years. I wish every musician could really feel that and just say, "Yes, I have to be who I am, I have to figure out what it is that is me," which is really hard. You can't look at yourself and say, "What do people love about me?" and when you first start out playing music you can't do that either. You can't tell, but if you do ever find out what it is, it always ends up being something that really surprises you. You have to do a lot of observing and listening.

I'm a singer who has no vibrato; I don't have the ability to do those big Celine Dion notes. My notes are singular, and they just sustain for a long way. It's like being a human firehose, with all that pressure behind you. What you can do is ride it and sculpt it while it's happening. When I listen to Die Kreuzen, and I listen to the way Dan sang, I can hear him doing that. It's such a specific thing, and there aren't a lot of singers out there who don't have vibrato, and it always made me feel like I was probably a really bad singer. All really good singers had it, and they could do it, but I couldn't. Dan doesn't have that. Dan has a very pure, gigantic-set-of-lungs kind of singing voice. I always thought I was lesser for that, but I feel very much like Die Kreuzen helped me find my voice. Listening to them made me feel like my friend had my back. I just felt so validated by them. I had the feeling listening to them that I later had when I was singing. It's really a crazy feeling when music actually changes your body to where your pulse and blood pressure rise, and you feel like you're doing something physical when you're listening. You feel the power of their instruments or their lungs.

David Pajo: Before Slint, I was in this band called Maurice, and the way our singer described us to people was that we sounded like a mixture of Metallica, Void, and Die Kreuzen. I don't think it was on purpose, but those were just the bands that we were all super into. They all had a similar melodic sensibility with all those diminished seventh chords. There were just certain chords that we'd call "evil chords," and a couple people did it, including Die Kreuzen. Neither Void nor Die Kreuzen were household names in '84 and '85, but for us they were. For us and all of our friends, they were gods [laughs].

They *still* are to me. They were so far ahead of their time, it's insane. Dan's vocals predate black metal, Keith's alternate picking basslines predate black metal—everything is just so far ahead. If you listen to the second wave of black metal, stuff like Mayhem and Darkthrone, to me they took elements of early Die Kreuzen and made it their own sound.

In some ways, "All White" is kind of like the first black-metal song. It speeds up to where it's almost that tempo, and Dan is doing the shrieking and the lyrics are so intense.

Greg Anderson: There's definitely black-metal musicians who are more open-minded than what you'd typically expect. The vocal style and the dissonance and atmosphere of the music Die Kreuzen made share a lot of similar characteristics of black metal.

David Pajo: I never got to see them, but later when I finally saw footage I just thought that the way Keith moved onstage was so cool. Whenever I get bored on stage or feel myself going through the motions with a band, I'll think about Keith and the way he moves on stage, and it will completely energize me. It's so incredible, and I don't really get that feeling from watching people usually. People just do their rock 'n' roll moves or whatever. I loved the way Angus and Malcolm Young got into it when they're on stage, but Keith Brammer is something else.

I talked about Die Kreuzen a lot during Slint, because I really liked the way they arranged their riffs. People used to tell me that Slint's guitar parts were really angular, and I never really knew what they meant by that, but I think it's mostly because of Brian Egeness's guitar playing. His playing is about as angular as it gets—it's like a kaleidoscope. When we were putting together Slint songs, I was always thinking about them, just like, "What would Die Kreuzen do?"

Matt Sweeney: Listen to Slint—it's totally colored by Die Kreuzen in the best way! It continued in that same tradition of taking your influences to a different place.

David Pajo: Every aspect of Die Kreuzen I just love. All the musicianship, the lyrics, the way they presented themselves—they were just worlds apart from everyone else. They were just one of those magic combinations of people.

Nathan Larson: Within Shudder to Think, we all loved Die Kreuzen, but for whatever reason we never really talked about them. We were taking the more mathy aspects of what they were doing a little bit further. There was stuff about what we were doing that was so parallel to what they were doing. The sensation of listening to Die Kreuzen was something I was trying to chase. This kind of soaring feeling but also this uncanny strangeness underneath it. It's this unplaceable kind of feeling.

John Reis: That first record really was an important record to me. It still is. It's a record I'll reference—I'll put it on when the mood strikes. It kinda ended up being one of those records that you show to your friend when you're trying to one-up them. "Oh, you think that's gnarly?" and then you play them the Die Kreuzen record and you're like, "*This* is fuckin' gnarly." Very few records have ever blown my mind the way that that record has.

Die Kreuzen was a huge influence on Pitchfork and Drive Like Jehu. We didn't really feel like we had too many kindred spirits until more bands started to form in San Diego.

Mario Rubalcaba (drummer, Clikatat Ikatowi, Earthless, Off!): The earliest version of Clikatat Ikatowi, we had a more arty approach to songwriting, and Die Kreuzen was definitely one of the first talking points between Scott and myself. Die Kreuzen was the one that was huge for us.

Justin Trosper: Unwound were tied pretty closely to the San Diego bands early on, and our roadie Dustin was tight with those guys. We'd play that first Die Kreuzen record in the van a lot. That first record was a big deal for a lot of those San Diego guys. Like the first time I heard Pitchfork, I remember thinking that Rick Froberg's voice kind of reminded me of Die Kreuzen in the way he was singing.

Mario Rubalcalba: Erik's drumming was super-influential to me. Bad Brains did that galloping-horses running type of beat, and Erik did his own version of that. He did a lot of those weird start/stop things, just lots of weird fills, but it always kept moving. It never slowed down, it always kept chugging along. It was really propulsive.

One of the first Clikatat Ikatowi songs we ever wrote was totally a Die Kreuzen–inspired song. If I had to get rid of all my records, the punk and hardcore section would become pretty slim, but there's no way I'm ever getting rid of that first Die Kreuzen record. Circle Jerks might have to leave, but Die Kreuzen is sticking around [laughs].

Nathan Larson: If you were into alternative rock in the '80s, it was a pretty small scene, and Die Kreuzen were one of the bands on the scene who were making these really cool records. A lot of key people who later went on to form bands were listening to them.

Justin Trosper: Looking at it now, Die Kreuzen totally helped invent the whole grunge thing. I know all those bands were into them. All the Midwest bands seem to be a major part of what eventually became the grunge thing that Seattle got famous for. Die Kreuzen, Soul Asylum, Hüsker Dü, and then some of the Chicago bands ... they were all kinda abrasive and had long hair and wore flannel shirts. They were doing all that before anyone in Seattle got credit for doing that. The Midwestern sensibility and style, I feel like *that's* where grunge came from.

If you look, they were wearing T-shirts from all those bands. All of those people saw them early on. I remember asking Tobi Vail from Bikini Kill, and she was telling me about how phenomenal they were. I feel like everyone who saw them felt that way, because of how energetic they were. When you watch videos of them, they're super-rockin', they're like headbanging, there's almost like a tiny bit of a metal vibe there. They were evolving out of that suburban super-fast punk thing and moving into these more complex and progressive song structures and breakdowns. They were doing things that were unconventional at the time.

Neko Case: When I saw them in Tacoma, there were a ton of people there who ended up forming the bands from the Pacific Northwest that a lot of people talk about. They had a very wide appreciation for music and Die Kreuzen was totally on their radar. I loved the first Soundgarden EP because it made me feel the same way that Die Kreuzen made me feel. When I think about them, I just think there's no way that they wouldn't have been influenced by them.

Greg Anderson: There's a mindset that I've taken from them. I've just been a mega-fan and have always tried to do a different version of music that I like. I take a lot of inspiration from very different and eclectic music. For Sunn O)), we're all super-obsessed with and influenced by jazz, like Eric Dolphy and John Coltrane and Miles Davis. We don't really sound like that at all, but it's the spirit of what they did, and the freeness and openness of that music is something we really connected with and try to channel in what we're doing.

What I love about Die Kreuzen is that they do the unexpected. It seemed to me that they were always trying to do something different on each record. Whenever I saw them, it was always not what I expected. I have so much respect for that. The music that Sunn O)) makes, we always try to make it different from what we did before. It's just part of our DNA—we want to keep pushing ourselves and push the boundaries as much as we possibly can. That's the inspiration that I draw from Die Kreuzen. With the live experience, too, we just try to make it to where it's something unexpected and be different from the concert we played the night before.

I love the dissonance and darkness of the music. That's something I've always been attracted to and drawn to. It's why I can still listen to that music today. It still makes me feel the same way I did when I first heard it so many years ago. There's a lot of records I can listen to now and like because they're nostalgic, but there's the next step of records where you gotta ask—does it hold up beyond that? There's a lot of older records that are just a nostalgic trip for me, something sentimental. There's a few records that go beyond that, that I still really connect with, in the headspace that I'm in now. That headspace has partially developed because of this music. They transcend the sentimental aspect and become part of your life and part of who you are.

John Reis: Brian's guitar playing has this atonal quality. I might evoke that in a different way, but that idea is the same thing, and I got that from Die Kreuzen. Letting different strings resonate, or putting in notes that don't necessarily fit, to where the notes kind of just rub against each other in a wrong way that sounds right—that's definitely something I got from them.

There's a Hot Snakes song called "Why Don't It Sink In?" that's completely our ode to Die Kreuzen. It's pretty obvious when you listen to it. Everyone in Hot Snakes loved Die Kreuzen.

Mario Rubacalba: The records just aren't dated at all. I relate to the energy of that stuff, whether it's coming from being a teenager and growing up with it or not. I still relate to those records, I still feel it. It doesn't feel like something I liked more as a kid—it still gets me a charge out of hearing it. There's this secret ingredient that some bands have that can only come from having a really good chemistry playing with each other. Die Kreuzen have that. Not every record or band is timeless, but the ones that are hit the jackpot.

Marilynn Mee: You think about the music that has withstood the test of time over decades and it's often the ones who just set out to do what they wanted to do—those are the ones who have become the most revered and respected. It's not the people who were trying to please the fans or figure out what song is gonna get the most airplay; it's the acts who are just truly and completely themselves that continue to connect with people

Above: Keith tears it up on stage at Stache's in Columbus, Ohio, in 1988. Photo: Jay Brown.

Below: The men in the trees? The band in Detroit during the *October File* era, c. 1985-86. Photo: Corey Rusk.

long after the fact. This is why Die Kreuzen continues to be as important as they are.

Nathan Larson: To have been young in the '80s was so great. We were given a huge gift to come of age in an era when we had bands like Sonic Youth and REM and Die Kreuzen and the Pixies. Anyone who was coming of age then and playing in bands, if you were really tuned in to what was going on, Die Kreuzen were one of *the* bands you were listening to. They were a really important part of my '80s experience. I've carried my copy of *October File* with me since I bought it in 1987. It's stayed with me through every single move, and I have such a soft spot for it. I have that whole record practically memorized. I played it for my son the other day, just super-loud on the turntable, and it sounded great. ●

Thank You: For many reasons, this book would not have been possible if not for Keith Brammer, Brian Egeness, Dan Kubinski, Erik Tunison, Richard Kohl, and Corey Rusk. Your patience, trust, and kindness are the reason why this book exists, and I can't express enough gratitude to the six of you. Karl Paloucek was able to finally track down Richard Kohl after many failed attempts on my end. Matt Stenger's now-defunct Die Kreuzen archive was a fantastic resource that helped me out immensely. Every additional interviewee in this book was incredibly generous with their time and helped this project become more than just a traditional band history. Finally, I'd like to thank Christina and Jessica at Feral House for their ongoing support over the last decade. Thank you for believing in this project.

Acknowledgements: My family, Morgan, all my friends, and Hrvoje Bubić.

A Complete Index of Voices

Keith Brammer: Bassist of Die Kreuzen.

Brian Egeness: Guitarist of Die Kreuzen.

Dan Kubinski: Singer of Die Kreuzen.

Erik Tunison: Drummer of Die Kreuzen.

Brian Beezer Hill: Bassist of the Stellas and member of Sacred Order.

Mary Jo Tunison: wife of Erik Tunison.

Richard Kohl: Graphic designer who created cover art for every Die Kreuzen release from *Cows and Beer* on. Kohl also managed the band for a brief time.

Damian Abraham: Vocalist for Fucked Up and host of the *Turned Out a Punk* podcast.

Michael Alago: A&R executive responsible for signing Metallica, White Zombie, Metal Church, and many other bands.

Steve Albini: Recording engineer and founder of Electrical Audio. Member of Big Black, Shellac, and other bands. Writer for numerous independent 'zines and publications.

Greg Anderson: Member of Engine Kid, Sunn O))), and Goatsnake, and co-founder of Southern Lord Records.

Lou Barlow: member of Deep Wound, Dinosaur Jr., and Sebadoh.

Janet Billig Rich: Former publicity and A&R at Caroline Records.

Rick Canzano: Recording engineer for Die Kreuzen's first two albums.

Neko Case: Singer/songwriter and member of the New Pornographers.

Mike Gitter: Founder of *xXx Fanzine*, music writer, VP of A&R at Century Media.

Nathan Larson: Member of Swiz and Shudder to Think.

Dennis Lyxzen: Vocalist for the bands Refused, the International Noise Conspiracy, and Fake Names.

Ian MacKaye: Member of Minor Threat and Fugazi and founder of Dischord Records.

Paul Mahern: Singer for the Zero Boys from Indianapolis, Indiana.

Marilyn Mee: Radio programmer, WLZR, Milwaukee, Wisconsin.

Thurston Moore: Guitarist for Sonic Youth.

Bob Nastanovich: Member of Pavement and Silver Jews.

David Pajo: Member of Slint, Yeah Yeah Yeahs, Interpol, Tortoise, and several others.

Jon Reis: Guitarist for Pitchfork, Drive Like Jehu, Rocket from the Crypt, Hot Snakes, and several others.

Mario Rubalcalba: Drummer for Clikatat Ikatowi, OFF!, and Earthless.

Corey Rusk: Bass Player for the Necros, co-founder of Touch and Go Records.

Matt Sweeney: Member of Chavez, Zwan, and the Hard Quartet.

Kim Thayil: Guitar player and founding member of Soundgarden.

Justin Trosper: Vocalist and guitarist for Olympia, Washington, post hardcore band Unwound.

Butch Vig: Drummer for Garbage. Producer for *Century Days*, "Gone Away," and *Cement*.

Brad Wood: Producer for Liz Phair, Placebo, Sunny Day Real Estate and many other bands.

Jon Wurster: Drummer for Superchunk, Bob Mould, Mountain Goats, and many other bands.

SATURDAY
MARCH
13
die
KREUZEN
w/ TENSE
EXPERTS

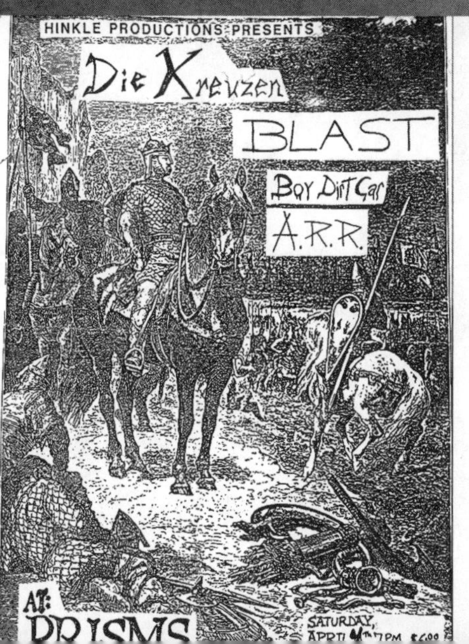

In Milwaukee, as in Los Angeles, the hardcore punk scene, a small but visible contingent centered mostly at the Starship Club, 635 N. 5th St., formed as a reaction to new wave's fashionable appeal.

"I hate all those new wave people who come down to the Starship all dressed up in their cute punk outfits with the attitude, 'Ooooo, let's go dancing,' " said Keith Brammer, from the Milwaukee hardcore punk band, Die Kreuzen, who plays tonight with the Zero Boys at the Starship.

Local variation

Die Kreuzen forms the local rallying point for Milwaukee hardcore followers. When Die Kreuzen, or Sacred Order, or Los Angeles bands like Fear, perform in Milwaukee, the hardcore crowd turns out to push around the dance floor in Milwaukee's version of slam dancing.

Participants ram and shove into each other in motions fitting what one observer called "a rugby scrimmage at Vince Lombardi High School."

The dance-floor crowd is usually leather-jacketed, generally in their late teens and early 20s and predominantly male. Most women and some small men have found the dance too rough for less muscular frames.

"I slam dance, but it depends on who else is on the dance floor," said Diane, 20. "Most people are out there to have fun. But some people try to act tough and throw punches.

"But I like hardcore because it's more a way of life. New wave is for dips."

Still, most deny that Milwaukee's scene holds the violent underbelly of Los Angeles.

"Some college kids off the football field walk in and they misinterpret the shoving," said Die Kreuzen vocalist Dan Kubinski. "They think you're supposed to kill each other. You're supposed to bounce into each other and have a good time. The music's really too fast to dance to it any oth-

Punk rock isn't dead yet

Milwaukee's punk band, Die Kreuzen: (from left) Keith Bramme, Brian Egeness, Dan Kubinski, Eric Tunison

THE MILWAUKEE JOURNAL Friday, April 9, 1982